TEACH YOUR CHILD SCIENCE

MAKING SCIENCE FUN FOR THE BOTH OF YOU

Michael Shermer

LOWELL HOUSE

Los Angeles

CONTEMPORARY BOOKS

Chicago

Library of Congress Cataloging-in-Publication Data

Shermer, Michael.
    Teach your child science.
      p.   cm.
    ISBN 0-929923-08-1
    1. Science—Study and teaching (Elementary)
    2. Education—Parent participation.   I. Title
    LB 1585.S46 1989   89-12534
    372.3 ' 5044—dc19   CIP

Lowell House
1875 Century Park East
Los Angeles, CA 90067

Design: MIKE YAZZOLINO
Manufactured in the United States of America
10   9   8   7   6   5   4   3   2   1

———————

This book is dedicated to those scientists who have had the will and courage to take time from their scholarly research to write for the general public about their life's passion. A child's initial encounter with science is almost always from such a book. It is these scientists who are shaping the minds of our future.

———————

Acknowledgments

I would like to acknowledge the valuable and comprehensive feedback offered by Paul MacCready. The extensive time he invested is indicative of his love of the scientific endeavor. Naturally I take full responsibility for any mistakes or misrepresentations. I also thank historian of science Richard Olson for expanding my understanding of science as a human and social enterprise. My editor Janice Gallagher was invaluable in helping me convert complex scientific and scholarly subjects into readable and comprehensible text. Her persistence and patience were indefatigable. Derek Gallagher, Amy Rudnick, and Mary Nadler were instrumental in producing a book that alleviated the fears all authors have of how the final product will look. And I thank Jack Artenstein for the opportunity in the first place.

Contents

―――――――――

"One thing I have learned in a long life: that all our science, measured against reality, is primitive and childlike—and yet it is the most precious thing we have."

ALBERT EINSTEIN

―――――――――

A Personal
Note to Parents

Several years ago I heard the famous astronomer and science popularizer Carl Sagan give a speech at the California Institute of Technology (Cal Tech). In that speech, Sagan clearly and succinctly stated a need in the scientific community:

> In exchange for freedom of inquiry, scientists are obliged to explain their work. If science is considered a closed priesthood, the dangers of abuse are greater. But if science is a topic of general interest and concern—if both its delights and its social consequences are discussed regularly and competently in the schools, the press, and at the dinner table—we have greatly improved our prospects for learning how the world really is and for improving both it and us.

This quote summarizes one of the three reasons why I have written this book. My reasons are as follows:

1. **To HELP PARENTS AND CHILDREN UNDERSTAND THE METHODS AND BENEFITS OF SCIENCE.**

As a college professor and historian of science, I feel a certain obligation to transcribe the sometimes arcane and obfuscating nature of science and the scientific method. In other words, I agree with Sagan and have responded to his challenge, especially with the possibility science and technology presents for improving the world and ourselves. The well-known psychologist B. F. Skinner once wrote: "The methods of science have been enormously successful wherever they have been tried. Let us then apply them to human affairs." Thus far the rules of the game of science have been played strictly and fairly within the realm of the physical and biological sciences, but when it comes to the social sciences, especially politics, the methods of science have been poorly employed. I believe that by teaching children the methods of science at an early age, we might enable them to apply the rules of science to human affairs when they grow up.

In addition, I would add that there is something sublime about science, something that is understood by all who play the game but that usually goes unspoken. When I was a child, like many children I had dreams, ambitions, and fantasies about my heroes and how I might grow up to be like them. Since I always liked history, I read of the travels and exploits and conquests of such great men as Alexander the Great, Julius and Augustus Caesar, and, especially, Napoleon. But as I grew up it became apparent that I would never have the opportunity to fill such enormous shoes, and I felt some disappointment.

When I discovered science, that disappointment was allayed. I never really understood why. It was just something that was written between the lines in the books of science and the biographies of scientists that I read. It had something to do with personal power and self-fulfillment in a cause bigger than life, a cause that no one hero could claim as his own. Much later I came to recognize this feeling when I read the following passage written by Alfred North Whitehead in reference to scientists from the time of Ancient Greece to the present:

> The great conquerors, from Alexander to Caesar, and from Caesar to Napoleon, influenced profoundly the lives of subsequent generations. But the total effect of this influence shrinks to insignificance, if compared to the entire transformation of human habits and human mentality produced by the long line of men of thought from Thales to the present day, men individually powerless, but ultimately the rulers of the world.

In this sublimity there is a goal that transcends all—the goal to understand the universe and everything in it. The renowned

British physicist Stephen Hawking, in his best-selling book *A Brief History of Time,* expressed this ambition: "Today we still yearn to know why we are here and where we came from. Humanity's deepest desire for knowledge is justification enough for our continuing quest. And our goal is nothing less than a complete description of the universe we live in."

2. TO STEM THE TIDE OF PSEUDOSCIENCE.

The second reason for my writing this book is a concern I have for an apparently rising tide of irrationality and interest in claims of the paranormal. Pseudoscience is flourishing while science, in many ways, seems to be floundering. I have read journal articles reporting that 52 percent of Americans believe in astrology, 46 percent think that ESP is real, and 35 percent believe that ghosts exist. Meanwhile, I get reports at the college where I teach from the Educational Testing Service (ETS) stating that the science literacy of American schoolchildren is at a level that is "depressing and alarming." ETS recently noted that "more than half of the nation's seventeen-year-olds are so poorly educated in science that they cannot benefit from special job training and cannot perform work requiring basic technical understanding." A mere *seven percent* scored high enough to perform adequately in college-level science courses.

The alarming news is not going away. The journal *Social Studies of Science,* for example, recently reported a study by the Massachusetts Institute of Technology concluding from a survey that one out of four Americans think that the sun is a planet, not a star, a mere 24 percent realize that the universe is expanding, and "only a third of American adults have a minimally acceptable understanding of the universe."

I believe that the solution to this two-edged problem (the rise of pseudoscience and the demise of science) must begin at home. Children do not suddenly become curious in the first grade. They begin wondering about the world and the things in it soon after birth.

The Japanese have figured this out. The April 17, 1989, edition of *Newsweek* reported that "Japanese students have the highest math and science test scores in the world." Why? "Parents, especially mothers, play a key role in education," the article reported. ". . . More than 80 percent of Japanese children learn to read or write to some extent before they enter school." The director of the National Institute for Educational Research reported: "It is as if mothers had their own built-in curriculum. The first game they teach is to count numbers up to 10."

These early years are critical in the nurturing of a scientific spirit in our nation's children. Yes, our schools need to offer a greater quantity and quality of scientific education, but let's not shirk our domestic duties.

3. TO CONVEY THE JOYS OF SCIENCE.

The third reason for my writing this book (and probably the strongest of the three) is far less virtuous. I confess with unabashed candidness that I just-plain-old *love* science and the scientific way of thinking, and I want to share that enthusiasm with as many people as possible. Science is fun. Science is like a game, and once you've learned the rules, you and your child can also play. Science offers the additional advantage of teaching us not only *what* to think about certain things, but also *how* to think about nearly everything. Science is not just things; it's thinking. And finally, science opens up the world, allowing us to befriend people around the globe. Science knows none of the barriers imposed by politics, religion, or race. The seventeenth-century astronomer Christiaan Huygens said, "The world is my country, science my religion."

There are lots of books on science. There are books for children on doing scientific experiments, and there are books for scholars and scientists (and serious amateurs) on the scientific method. This book attempts to fill a gap by offering parents and children a book on the methods of science, or the science of understanding. My goal is to help parents teach their children how to think scientifically, not just to conduct experiments willy-nilly, with no understanding of why the experiments are done. Theories without experiments are hollow, but experiments without theories are meaningless. *Doing* science without *understanding* science is like playing tennis without a net or out-of-bounds lines. A goal of this book is to provide parents and children the net and boundaries for the game of science.

PART
ONE

Getting Excited About Science

"To myself I seem to have been only like a boy playing on the seashore, and diverting myself and now and then finding a smoother pebble or a prettier shell than ordinary, while the great ocean of truth lay all undiscovered before me."

SIR ISAAC NEWTON

1

Every Child as Scientist

On the opening page of a splendid little book by the biologist Vincent Dethier called *To Know a Fly*, the author makes this humorous observation of how children grow up to become scientists: "Although small children have taboos against stepping on ants because such actions are said to bring on rain, there has never seemed to be a taboo against pulling off the legs or wings of flies. Most children eventually outgrow this behavior. Those who do not either come to a bad end or become biologists."

Something happens to many children between the early years when they are knowledge junkies and the time that they graduate from high school. Something in our society squelches the curiosity of many a child. But not all. Those who remain curious don't, in a sense, grow up, or they may grow up to become scientists. In fact, the famous student of animal behavior Niko Tinbergen says that "the scientist, because of his eager curiosity, at times appears childish to others." In other words, a scientist is really a child inside, and children are really just little scientists.

When we are born we have no cultural experience whatsoever. But we do not come into the world completely ignorant. We know lots of things—such as how to see, how to hear, how to digest food, and so on. We also inherit what our ancestors experienced through millions of years of evolution in a world filled with predators and natural disasters, poisons and dangers, and risks from all sides. The fact that we are here is a testimony to their ability to understand and interpret the world around them, for understanding what is happening in your immediate world helps you to survive.

In a nutshell, the fundamental premise of all of science is this: it is an attempt to understand the causes of things. We are born with the ability to understand cause-and-effect relationships. For example, when babies crawl out over a ledge onto a piece of transparent glass, they become very anxious and immediately crawl back to "solid" ground. Babies are born with the knowledge that ledges are dangerous places. When we eat something noxious, we usually never desire it again. This is called "taste aversion" or "one-trial learning." In the natural environment, things we eat that make us sick are likely to be poisonous and should not be tried again. This is the process of understanding cause-and-effect relationships at a most fundamental level.

Our brains are natural machines for piecing together events that may be related and for solving problems that require our attention. One can envision an ancient hominid from Southern Africa chipping and grinding and shaping a rock into a sharp tool for carving up a giant mammalian carcass. Or perhaps we can imagine the first individual who discovered that knocking flint and steel together would create a spark with which to start a fire. The wheel, the lever, the bow and arrow, the plow—inventions intended to allow us to shape our environment rather than simply be shaped by it—started the history of civilization down a path that led to our modern scientific and technological world. So we, and our children, are the descendents of the most successful individuals at understanding and manipulating the environment.

Children are natural-born scientists. They are curious, inquisitive, and full of vim and vigor in the exploration of their world. Children want to know everything, and if they find someone who knows *anything*—usually beginning with mom and dad—the questions begin, and seemingly never end. Why is the sky blue? What is wind? Why is it cold in the winter and hot in the summer? What makes it rain? Like our ancestors, children begin with questions about the natural environment. It's normal to want to know how things work and why the world is the way it is. At its most basic level, this is what science is all about. And scientists are just professionals at doing what children do so naturally. But scientists do more than just *ask* questions; they also try to answer them using the scientific method, which will be addressed in the next chapter.

Perhaps an example can help explain what I mean when I say that children are scientists, and what you can do to nourish that potential in your child.

The famous physicist Richard Feynman was one of those curious characters who never grew up. Among his many contributions to science, Dr. Feynman worked on the Manhattan Project during World War II, helping to build the atomic bomb, won the Nobel Prize in Physics in 1965, and was a professor of Physics at the prestigious California Institute of Technology in Pasadena, California (where his lectures in physics became so well known that they were published in three volumes in 1965 as the famous *Feynman Lectures in Physics*).

Feynman's brilliance and creativity do not end there. The subtitle of his very popular book *Surely You're Joking, Mr. Feynman* is *The Adventures of a Curious Character.* And a curious character Feynman certainly was. He never went a day without being curious about something to the point of investigating it further. For example, he picked top-secret government safes at Los Alamos (just for fun), discussed particle physics with hookers in a taxicab in Las Vegas, played drums in a band, composed music for a ballet, learned to draw respectable portraits, learned a foreign language well enough to deliver a physics paper in that language at a conference in a foreign country, and delivered a lecture on physics with Albert Einstein in the audience!

Feynman was the consummate scientist—curious about everything, closed-minded to nothing, willing to try almost anything. And to refresh your memory of more recent scientific history, it was Feynman who exposed the discovery that the O rings in the space shuttle *Challenger* failed because of the cold weather, resulting in the disastrous explosion that killed all seven astronauts aboard. Feynman's simple experiment of dipping a piece of an O ring in a glass of ice water during the investigative-committee meeting convinced the other members that this is where the blame was to be placed for the tragedy.

In Feynman's most recent (and posthumously published) book, *What Do You Care What Other People Think?*, he explains in the first chapter ("The Making of a Scientist") the events in his childhood that shaped him into a scientist. Psychologists now know that parental influence is a critical and vital force in the creation of a child's personality. Feynman's father told his mother before the boy was born, "If it's a boy, he's going to be a scientist." The father's dreams could not have been more fulfilled. (Feynman also has a sister with a Ph.D. in physics.) Feynman tells a story that is emblematic of the type of teaching a parent can do with a child to encourage scientific thinking:

> We had the *Encyclopaedia Britannica* at home. When I was a small boy [my father] used to sit me on his lap and read to me from the *Britannica*. We would be reading, say, about dinosaurs. It would say something like, "This dinosaur is twenty-five feet high and its head is six feet across." My father would stop reading and say, "Now, let's see what that means. That would mean that if he stood in our front yard, he would be tall enough to put his head through our window up here." (We were on the second floor.) "But his head would be too wide to fit in the window." Everything he read to me he would translate as best he could into some reality. It was very exciting and very, very interesting to think there were animals of such magnitude—and that they all died out, and that nobody knew why. I wasn't frightened that there would be one coming in my window as a consequence of this. But I learned from my father to translate: everything I read I try to figure out what it really means.

Learning "what it really means" in science cannot be overstressed. Almost anyone can memorize facts, but without the underlying principles the details are hollow. Facts and principles are the stone and mortar of science. Without the mortar, however, the edifice of science cannot be built. Feynman tells a story of how his father taught him "very early the difference between knowing the name of something and knowing something" when he was playing in a field with some kids:

> One kid says to me, "See that bird? What kind of bird is that?"
> I said, "I haven't the slightest idea what kind of a bird it is."
> He says, "It's a brown-throated thrush. Your father doesn't teach you anything!"
> But it was the opposite. He had already taught me: "See that bird?" he says. "It's a Spencer's warbler." (I knew he didn't know the real name.) "Well, in Italian, it's a *Chutto Lapittida*. In Por-

tuguese, it's a *Bom da Peida*. In Chinese, it's a *Chung-long-tah*, and in Japanese, it's a *Katano Tekeda*. You can know the name of that bird in all the languages of the world, but when you're finished, you'll know absolutely nothing whatever about the bird. You'll only know about humans in different places, and what they call the bird. So let's look at the bird and see what it's *doing*—that's what counts."

It doesn't take a scientist father or mother to create such examples. A few basic principles gleaned from an encyclopedia will do. The entire second section of this book is designed to help you to "do" science with your child. Even such important scientific laws as the ones that Newton discovered can be explained with the simplest of experiments. For example, as a young boy, Feynman discovered an understanding of Newton's first law (the law of inertia, where "every body continues in its state of rest, or of uniform motion in a right line, unless it is compelled to change that state by forces impressed upon it") while playing with his wagon:

My father taught me to notice things. One day, I was playing with an "express wagon," a little wagon with a railing around it. It had a ball in it, and when I pulled the wagon, I noticed something about the way the ball moved. I went to my father and said, "Say, Pop, I noticed something. When I pull the wagon, the ball rolls to the back of the wagon. And when I'm pulling it along and I suddenly stop, the ball rolls to the front of the wagon. Why is that?"

"That, nobody knows," he said. "The general principle is that things which are moving tend to keep on moving, and things which are standing still tend to stand still, unless you push them hard. This tendency is called 'inertia,' but nobody knows why it's true." Now, that's a deep understanding. He didn't just give me the name.

He went on to say, "If you look from the side, you'll see that it's the back of the wagon that you're pulling against the ball, and the ball stands still. As a matter of fact, from the friction it starts to move forward a little bit in relation to the ground. It doesn't move back."

I ran back to the little wagon and set the ball up again and pulled the wagon. Looking sideways, I saw that indeed he was right. Relative to the sidewalk, it moved forward a little bit.

So even toys, games, and everyday events can be used to explain scientific principles and the scientific way of thinking. You can develop this special kind of relationship with your child. For Feynman, that special relationship with his father led to a lifetime of curiosity and rewarding scientific advances: "That's the way I was educated by my father, with those kinds of examples and discussions: no pressure—just lovely, interesting discussions. It motivated me for the rest of my life, and it makes me interested in *all* the sciences."

Because of his upbringing, Feynman never really "grew up," in the way that a child holds an unmitigated quest to know and understand the world: "I've been caught, so to speak—like someone who was given something wonderful when he was a child, and he's always looking for it again. I'm always looking, like a child, for the wonders I know I'm going to find—maybe not every time, but every once in a while."

This book was written with the goal of teaching you how to teach your child science, how to give your child "something wonderful" so that he will always be "looking for it again." You never know—you just might be the parent of a future Nobel Prize winner!

The prime goal, however, is not for you to teach your child *what* to think so much as *how* to think—scientifically. If you tried to teach your child what to think, it would literally take forever. But if you teach your child how to think, he can figure out for himself what to think. A few basic thinking skills learned from doing science are all he needs to get started. These thinking skills will be covered in chapters 2, 3, and 4.

And the lesson may, at times, be reversed. In teaching your child science, you yourself may see science in a fresh and exciting new light. The questions children ask and the answers given to them will open doors for both parties. The question-and-answer style of teaching—the "Socratic method"—is a dialogue, not a monologue. For you to teach science, you must first understand the concept yourself. It is to this end that I have tried to convey the basics of science in a clear and straightforward manner, with hands-on examples and interactive games to be used to explain science to children. This first part, "Getting Excited about Science," is an important step for both you and your child. What science is and what science isn't are explained in the rest of this section, along with some of the rules of this special "game" you will be playing with your child.

Part Two presents information about "doing" science in a manner that will allow you and your child to learn together, conducting simple experiments that demonstrate the principles of science. That part will show you how to teach children the joys and wonder of the world of science. The ability to wonder, and to be persistent in that wondering, is at the heart of the scientific spirit. As Feynman wrote as a young boy:

> I wonder why I wonder why,
> I wonder why I wonder.
> I wonder why I wonder why,
> I wonder why I wonder.

CHAPTER
2

Science as a Game: What Science Is

Many people are intimidated by science, since scientists and their work often seem far removed from the everyday things of our world. But science need not be intimidating. In fact, science can be defined in the following way:

Science is a game for understanding the world, played by special rules called the scientific method.

Before you learn these rules, you and your child can do a simple scientific experiment to analyze how the game is played. This will also demonstrate how nonthreatening science can be. The game of science usually begins with a question that we want to answer. For example, a couple of thousand years ago Aristotle said that heavy objects fall faster than light objects. Is this true?

Take two balls—say, a baseball and a shot used in shot-putting. Obviously, if Aristotle is right, the shot should hit the ground before the baseball. Intuitively, this seems right. Hold both objects up as high as you can, and ask your child to notice which one hits the ground first when you let them go.

Now let them go simultaneously. Your child's answer should be that the balls hit the ground at the same time.

I just performed this experiment myself, and that appears to be what happened. (Make *sure* that you drop them at the same

10

time. The margin for error in this experiment is slim, to say the least. One scientist recently discovered that in this sort of experiment the *lighter* ball actually hit first, because it took people slightly longer to release the heavier ball: they had to hold the heavier ball tighter!)

It may take several tries before the effect is seen. Is it possible that the difference is so subtle that the experiment works only when the objects fall a long way? We'll do another experiment to answer this question. Stand up on a high object—a ladder, or the roof of your house—and let both objects go simultaneously. You'll need an assistant for this one, and your child will do just fine. Let both objects go, and ask her which one hits first. Again, she should find that they hit the ground at the same time. So far, so good. It appears that all objects fall at the same speed.

Your child may now ask an important question, and if she doesn't, you can. What if you drop a shot and a Ping-Pong ball? According to our findings so far, they should hit the ground at the same time. Do the experiment now. What did you discover?

So there is another aspect of the gravity experiment we didn't think of before. Air resistance can retard falling speed with objects that are very light or that have a broad surface area, such as a piece of paper or a feather. If we dropped a shot and a feather in a vacuum, would they hit at the same time? The experiment that would answer this question would be dropping the shot and a feather in a vacuum. Since it's probably safe to assume that few of us have access to a vacuum, we will have to turn to others who have already performed this experiment. (We can't check everything ourselves, so we must sometimes rely on others whose scientific methods we trust.) Scientists at Cal Tech have conducted a similar experiment, dropping a penny and a feather together in a vacuum chamber—and lo and behold, they hit the ground at the same time! You may also recall watching on television as one of the Apollo astronauts dropped a rock and a feather on the moon. Since the moon has no air, the rock and feather hit at the same time—hard to believe, but true.

As we have just seen, an experiment can be quite simple. You and your child will be conducting many such experiments in chapter 5. The point here is to eliminate any fears about science that may exist. Even a sophisticated and scholarly definition of science, when dismantled, turns out to be something any of us can understand. For example, science historian Richard Olson defines science in this way: "Science is a set of activities and habits of mind aimed at contributing to an organized, universally valid, and testable body of knowledge about phenomena."

This definition may seem complex and wordy, but let's take it apart and see what it really means. Science is a "set of activities." In other words, science is what scientists do. On a daily basis, for a living, in going about their business, scientists do science. Their activities are involved with science and the methods of science. "Habits of mind," however, implies that science is more than just *doing* something. Science is also a way of thinking. It is a way of interpreting the world that goes beyond the job or laboratory or classroom. We all have habits of mind. Scientists have a *particular* habit of mind—the habit of thinking scientifically, which is what you will be teaching your child to do. "Organizing knowledge" is nothing new. Everyone organizes knowledge every day. This is how we keep track of things in our minds, so scientists are just doing what we all do.

More important, science is "universally valid." That is, it doesn't depend on one person, or a group of people, or a particular laboratory that is doing the science. Objects of different weights tend to fall at the same speed when you drop them together and they do so in America, Russia, and Africa, as well as on the moon, Mars, and Pluto. The laws of gravity are "universally valid." We may not all agree on how well we like a certain painting, or what that painting might be worth, or what it means, but virtually everyone agrees that objects of different weights tend to fall at the same speed when you drop them. This is a primary difference between art and science. Art is subjective, and "beauty is in the eye of the beholder." By being universally valid, scientific phenomena do *not* depend on the beholder.

How does something become universally valid? By being "testable." The idea of falling objects is a testable one, and when the experiment is conducted as described above, the objects will hit the ground at the same time. The set of activities and the habits of mind that you and your child used in conducting the experiments on gravity showed you that the scientific idea of gravity is testable, universally valid, and, when described by mathematical formulas, part of *organized knowledge*. You and your child have just played the game of science that is played in this manner by all scientists—even Nobel Prize winners.

Olson's definition of science, of course, is not one you would read to your child. So let's return to our original definition, one you *can* use with your child: *Science is a game for understanding the world, played by special rules called the scientific method.* Let's now look at some of the rules and characteristics of this game of science.

THE RULES OF THE GAME

Although it is natural for children to wonder and be curious and ask lots of questions, they are not born knowing the rules of the game of science. For a game to be played correctly and fairly, the rules must be followed. Keep these rules in mind when you and your child do the experiments in chapter 5. Sometimes the rules are subtle and are learned as much by doing as by explaining. If your child has difficulty understanding some of the rules, understanding may come through participation as the two of you do the experiments. The rules themselves have been expressed in language that a child will understand. The examples I give of the rules in action are for your understanding. Following the rule I've included a section called "To Your Child" to help you explain the rule. Please note that these rules are *ideals* toward which science strives. But since science is a dynamic *human* and cultural enterprise, there are exceptions to the rules. Here are a few that most scientists feel are extremely important:

Rule 1: Honesty Is the Best Policy

We might also call this "Feynman's rule." Honesty is not something that anyone ever teaches you in science. It's just understood through the principles of the scientific method that those doing science will be honest. Feynman says that "it's a kind of scientific integrity, a principle of scientific thought that corresponds to a kind of utter honesty—a kind of leaning over backwards." When you and your child do experiments together, you'll know what Feynman means. It's not just not cheating (see Rule 2); it's going out of your way to make sure you've done everything right. For example, Feynman says, "If you're doing an experiment, you should report everything that you think might make it invalid— not only what you think is right about it: other causes that could possibly explain your results; and things you thought of that you've eliminated by some other experiment, and how they worked— to make sure the other fellow can tell they have been eliminated."

So the first rule is what Feynman calls "scientific integrity." It's being honest enough to tell others everything you know about your experiment. The experiment will be repeated by others. In the end, at least in science, the truth always comes out; if you haven't been honest, you won't get a good reputation as a scientist.

To your child (in your own words):

Do you remember that we talked about lying, and about how some people tell lies to get what they want? Well, scientists don't lie. Scientists try to be honest. Honesty is the best policy in the game of science. The reason for this rule is that scientists talk to one another a lot, and they tell one another what their experiments are like. If they lied about their experiments, then no one would believe them if they discovered something really exciting. Scientists try to tell other scientists *everything* they are doing, so that everyone can play the game better.

Rule 2: Cheating Is Not Allowed

With Rule 1, it is pretty obvious that cheating is not allowed. In other words, the scientist is not allowed to make up results. Furthermore, the scientist's personal beliefs, hopes, wishes, and desires should *not* affect the outcome of the game. It shouldn't matter who it is dropping two objects—you, I, or Albert Einstein would all get the same results.

However, expectations can influence results. One dramatic example of *subjectivity* in science was discovered by Harvard biology professor Stephen Jay Gould, when he retested some experiments done in the late 1800s on intelligence and skull size. It was believed then that the larger the brain the more intelligent the person, and that different races had different-size skulls (whites having the largest and blacks the smallest, with American Indians in between). Skull size can be measured by filling an empty skull with some material—say, mustard seed—and then pouring it back out into a container that gives a reading of the "cranial capacity." This was done in America by a medical doctor named Samuel Morton, and, sure enough, he discovered that whites had the largest brains, American Indians the next size down, and blacks the smallest. Over a century later Gould remeasured the skulls, this time using BB shot instead of mustard seed (BB shot is more *objective* because, unlike mustard seed, it can't be squashed down or shaken loose). Gould discovered virtually no differences among the skulls. Did Morton "cheat" on his data? Maybe, but Gould doesn't think so. Instead, Gould thinks that the expectation of finding differences was so strong that Morton actually found those differences. Gould concluded:

> Plausible scenarios are easy to construct. Morton, measuring by seed, picks up a threateningly large black skull, fills it lightly and gives it a few desultory shakes. Next, he takes a distressingly small Caucasian skull, shakes hard, and pushes mightily at the foramen magnum [the hole at the base of the skull] with his thumb. It is easily done, without conscious motivation; expectation is a powerful guide to action.

Ideally, science tries to avoid these problems, and the methodology of science helps detect human error. But the fact that they do happen tells us that science is not perfect. Rule 2 is a rule that we strive to follow, even if we don't always succeed.

To your child:

Cheating is never allowed in any game. Do you know why? When people cheat, it isn't fair for the other players who are playing the game fairly. What if everyone cheated? Then there wouldn't really be a game. Scientists are *never* supposed to cheat. If they do, and they get caught, it's much worse than cheating in a game at home. They can lose their jobs and not ever be allowed to play the game of science again.

Rule 3: Don't Take Another Person's Word for Something— Check It Out Yourself

One of the standard methods of finding things out is to ask others, especially if they are authorities. We may look to an authoritative book, such as the Bible, for final answers and indisputable truths. This is not always the case in science. While science does have its authorities, like Isaac Newton and Albert Einstein, scientists do not blindly follow them. In fact, a scientist primarily gains reputation and fame by being creative and original—which usually entails challenging existing authorities.

Children tend to be natural challengers to authority. Most children want to see something for themselves. Harry Truman used to say, "Show me—I'm from Missouri." Scientists say "Show me—I'm a scientist." This is a good way to start the training process for your child to be a scientist, so don't discourage such challenges by answering questions with something like "Because that's what scientists say." Scientists are frequently wrong. In conducting the experiment with falling objects, you and your child challenged Aristotle, one of the greatest authorities of all time. Galileo challenged him with this experiment, but you never know whether your child might be the next Galileo.

To your child:

Remember the experiment we did earlier, when we dropped the two balls and they hit at the same time? Well, a long time ago a really famous scientist named Aristotle said that the heavier ball would hit sooner than the light ball. If everyone believed Aristotle, then everyone would be wrong. Scientists don't believe in someone just because he's famous or important. Scientists like to see things for themselves. A scientist's two favorite words are "show me." [Have your child repeat these words.] Galileo was one of the first scientists who had the courage to challenge Aristotle. And Galileo turned out to be right. Maybe you'll grow up to be a really famous scientist like Galileo.

(To be fair to Aristotle, experimentation was not part of the scientific method and scientists didn't do these sorts of tests.)

Rule 4: Scientists Use Past Discoveries to Improve the Game

Science, like all games, changes and gets better over time. In the early days of the game of baseball, for example, participants played in run-down old parks with small gloves and crummy little wooden sticks. Now they play in big beautiful stadiums with huge gloves, composite baseball bats, and specially designed baseballs. Science is the same way. Scientists a hundred years ago had "run-down" equipment compared to what scientists use today. But as the game progressed and the rules were refined, scientists became better players.

Scientists today build on the knowledge discovered by scientists in the past. Before Copernicus theorized that the earth goes around the sun, for example, nearly everyone believed that the earth was stationary and that the sun, moon, planets, and stars all revolved around it. And this made a lot of sense. It's the way it looks and is the most obvious explanation. Think about it for a minute, and then ask your child: Do you *feel* the earth move? Can you see the earth move? Does it look like the sun goes around the earth? Every morning you and your child see the sun come up in the east and in the evening it seems to go down in the west. The next morning it comes back up in the east. It *appears* that the sun goes around the earth. Well, in spite of this, we know different today. We play the game with more skill now.

This rule also applies to what you are doing right now—teaching your child science. In a five-minute experiment with falling objects, you did what took past scientists centuries to figure out. In chapter 5, you and your child will perform another simple experiment to prove Newton's third law. ("To every action there is always opposed an equal reaction.") This law was the culmination of centuries of work by scientists, and Newton is hailed as one of the greatest scientists who ever lived. Yet you and your child can understand Newton's laws, without knowing any math, in a matter of minutes. The game of science is cumulative.

To your child:

[Start off by bringing up a game that your child likes to play, such as baseball or Monopoly.] Have you gotten better at this game since you first started playing? Of course you have, because whenever you play a game a lot, you get better. Scientists try to improve the game of science. They practice and improve, and as the game goes along, everyone gets better because they all help one another by being honest and not cheating. In fact, scientists use things that other scientists discovered in the past so that they don't have to start the game all over. For example, a long time ago people believed that the earth was flat. But now we know that it is round like a ball. We know because the shadow of the earth on the moon is round; and ships sailing out to sea slowly disappear, they don't just fall off; and we've seen pictures from space. Science has made lots of progress.

Rule 5: Try to Find "Natural" Answers to Questions

By "natural" answers, I mean answers that can be understood through things that can be observed by the senses—things that we can see, hear, touch, feel, or taste. Natural answers are practical, commonsense answers. If someone claims to have the ability to make an elephant disappear, scientists assume that this person is a good magician and can make the elephant disappear through magic. If the person claims to have "supernatural" powers, such as psychic ability, that can make an elephant disappear, scientists are skeptical, because this is not a natural explanation.

Another example is that of unidentified flying objects (UFOs). Natural explanations to account for sightings include planes, rockets, atmospheric disturbances, unusual cloud formations, our eyes tricking us, our memories becoming confused with dreams, and so on. Supernatural explanations usually involve creatures from another planet. As the head of the Southern California Skeptics, Al Seckel, says, "Before something can be claimed to be *out* of this world, you must first be absolutely sure that it's not *of* this world."

It's not that supernatural explanations are wrong and natural ones right. It's just that we need to check for natural reasons first. For example, we could call the air force or the local missile-launching site and ask if there was a flight over the area where a UFO was spotted, or we could check the weather service for any unusual atmospheric disturbances in the area.

Pre-industrial and aboriginal societies that don't have a systematic science frequently explain natural phenomena, such as lightning, by attributing the act to a god. This is a supernatural explanation. Children might do the same because they are scared or confused. One way to eliminate this fear is to give a natural explanation to your child.

For example, a quick glance at an encyclopedia such as the *Britannica* will help you to explain that lightning is a "visible discharge of atmospheric electricity that occurs when a region of the atmosphere acquires an electrical charge, or potential difference, sufficient to overcome the resistance of the air." This electrical charge is released from cloud to cloud or from cloud to ground. The thunder associated with lightning is caused by the "rapid heating of air to high temperatures along the whole length of the lightning channel. The air thus heated expands at supersonic speeds, but within a metre or two the shock wave decays into a sound wave, which is then modified by the intervening medium of air. . . . The result is a series of claps and rumbles." It's a little like discharging static electricity after rubbing your feet on the carpet and touching someone else. In the case of lightning the charge is tens of thousands of times greater, and so is the sound.

Of course, you wouldn't explain all this to your child in this manner, but might try something like this:

To your child:

[First generate a static spark by rubbing your feet on the carpet and touching a doorknob. Your child will see and hear the spark.] Lightning is electricity, just like the spark on the doorknob. The difference is that lightning is thousands of times more powerful than this little spark, therefore it is thousands of times brighter and louder.

It's not hard to use natural explanations, and they will remove a lot of childhood fears.

Rule 6: Arguments Are Usually Settled with Evidence, Not with Insults

Scientists may argue among themselves about the correctness of a theory or the validity of a hypothesis, but these arguments will be decided by scientific evidence and laboratory data, not by shouting or by hurling insults. Artists may argue whether one painting is better than another. But how could one ever decide? There is no experiment to perform and no test to conduct that would give us an answer. Art is subjective, and science has nothing to say about it. Therefore, artists can attack one another and art critics can criticize an artist's painting, because it's just opinion, after all.

The same is true of religion. There is no way to ever truly settle a religious dispute, because there is no scientific method by which we can determine which religion has the "right" god. The fact that there are thousands of different religions is a testimony to this fact. In the United States alone there are more than 1500 different "official" religions, nearly every one of which claims to be the "right" one. Since they contradict one another they can't all be right.

This is why science is such a great game for kids to learn. The sooner we can get more kids thinking scientifically, the sooner we can begin to rid the world of condemnation, unfair judging of others, attacks on people, and everyone claiming to be right in situations where there is in fact no way to settle the dispute. Science merely examines things the way they are. Disputes are settled in laboratories, journals, and books with experiments, data, and evidence—not on the battlefield with guns, bombs, and missiles.

To your child:

Have you ever had friends who got mad at each other and called each other names? Or do you remember seeing people on television trying to solve arguments by yelling at each other or shooting at each other? Scientists are not supposed to act this way. Scientists usually don't yell at each other or call each other names. They don't get in fights or try to hurt other scientists, because they would be breaking this rule. The reason is that the game of science is decided by experiments and evidence, not by yelling and fists and guns. Scientists decide who is right or wrong by looking at a scientist's experiments. Wouldn't it be great if the political leaders of America and Russia were scientists? Wouldn't it be great if the game of politics were played by the same rules as the game of science?

Rule 7: Nothing Is Ever Known for Sure in Science

It may seem strange to have a rule that says that nothing is known for sure in this game, but that's what makes science such a fun game to play. You never know what's going to happen next! Since nothing is known for certain, nothing in science can be proved 100 percent. Science is conducted by scientists, who, like all people, have personal beliefs that may cause them to make mistakes. We were pretty certain that the space shuttle would never blow up, yet it did. In 1901 one of the most renowned physicists in history, William Thomson (better known as Lord Kelvin), "proved" that humans would never be able to fly a heavier-than-air craft. After the Wright brothers proved *him* wrong in 1903, he published another paper "proving" that airplanes would never be able to carry heavy loads and were therefore not commercially practical. As I've said, nothing is certain in science.

To your child:

Do you know people who think they know everything? But they *don't* know everything, do they? Nobody knows everything. A very famous scientist once said he could prove airplanes could never fly. But the Wright brothers proved that scientist wrong. One of the rules of science is that nothing is ever known for sure. Nobody is a "know-it-all" in science. Scientists all work together to try to play the game better, but they know that no matter what they discover, it might turn out to be wrong, or maybe not completely wrong, but not exactly right.

Of course, as we saw in Rule 4, science does make progress and thus builds confidence. If differently weighted balls fall at the same speed in a thousand experiments, we become very confident that they will do so again in the next experiment.

Rule 8: There Are No Secrets in Science

Scientists are proud to publish their results in journals and books. In fact, this is how they get raises and promotions. As we saw in Olson's definition of science, science is "testable." Scientists can test the results obtained by another scientist only if they know *exactly* what the other scientist did to get his or her results. Therefore, scientific journals are highly detailed, with lots of graphs, charts, and numbers provided so that the experimenter can explain how the experiment was done.

For example, I worked for a couple of years in an experimental psychology laboratory, trying to determine how people and animals make choices. I was curious as to how a choice is made—whether it's based on how much of something you get, or on the quality of it, or whatever. I gave rats a choice between two different quantities of sugar water, one very sweet and the other not as sweet. (Rats, like most mammals, including—and especially—people, love sugar, even if it is not especially good for them!) The rats pressed one of two different bars to trigger a mechanism that lifted a little drinking cup up. Then I varied the choices by giving them twice the amount of sugar on the right to see if they would press that bar twice as many times. I also varied how many bar presses it took to get a drink (for example, making it necessary for the rat to press the right bar twice as many times as the left to get the same sugar solution). I added another factor by putting salt in one of the sugar solutions so that it didn't taste as good, thus making it qualitatively different, and so on. (Later I did a similar choice experiment on people, but with different choices.)

I found that the rats tended to match the number of bar presses to the percentage of sugar in the solution, the frequency they got to drink, and the quality (no salt versus salt). I devised a mathematical formula to describe this phenomenon, called the "matching law," and published the results. Since anyone who wanted to check my results would have to perform the experiment *exactly* as I did, in my paper I had to explain *exactly* how I mixed the sugar in the water, what kind of sugar I used and what percentage of the solution it was, how big the cage was, how much I fed the rats each day (hunger could affect the results), what type of lighting I used in the rat cage, what the room temperature was, what electrical apparatus I used, what type of rats was involved, how much they weighed each day . . . you get the picture.

To your child:

You know how people have secrets? Well, sometimes secrets are okay. There are some things that I tell you that are secret and just between you and me. Or maybe you and a friend have some secrets between each other that you don't want others to know about. These are okay, too. But scientists don't have secrets when they are playing the game of science. In fact, they try to tell one another everything they are doing so that they can all play the game better. Because of this, the game of science moves very fast—faster than other games in life. Scientists also make friends with other scientists around the world, because even if those other scientists are from different countries or belong to a different race, they are friends because they don't have secrets.

It should be noted that the ideal of this rule is changing with the development of "proprietary science," where laboratories are privately owned and scientific discoveries are potentially patentable, thus profitable, and therefore kept secret from other such labs.

Rule 9: Scientists Admit When They're Wrong

Because science is testable, scientists frequently repeat experiments that other scientists do. Usually, if a scientist has done his or her research carefully, other scientists will get the same or very similar results. But occasionally, different results are obtained. This sets off an alarm: Did the scientist make a mistake? Did his assistants make mistakes? Did he lie or make up his data? Did he have an unconscious bias?

This really does happen in science. As we saw earlier, when Gould reproduced Morton's skull experiments he got different results and concluded that Morton's expectation had influenced his results. When I was in graduate school in psychology, it was discovered that a famous British psychologist named Cyril Burt had actually faked his data in some studies of twins having to do with the inheritability of IQ.

Biases and forgeries do occur in science, and scientists, like everyone else, make mistakes. But the important thing in science is that mistakes are corrected. Scientists admit when they're wrong. Scientists catch one another's mistakes or biases, and they expose those who cheat. And scientists really do change their minds when new evidence presents itself. It's not always easy, but they do it. For example, a friend of Charles Darwin's named Charles Lyell didn't believe that Darwin's new theory of evolution applied to humans. For many years, in fact, Lyell was quite open about opposing his friend on this point. But as more and more evidence presented itself, Lyell eventually changed his mind, admitting that Darwin was probably right.

To your child:

One of the hardest things for any of us to do is to admit when we are wrong. It's hard because it makes us feel bad when we are wrong, and no one likes to feel bad. But scientists have to learn to play the game with this rule and to overcome those bad feelings. If they don't, they are breaking the rule, and other scientists will get mad at them for not admitting they were wrong. In fact, being wrong is actually a good part of the game. When you are wrong a lot, it means you've been trying. And if you've been trying a lot, then you will also be right sometimes. In baseball, Babe Ruth was the greatest home-run hitter in the game. He also struck out more than anyone else. All great scientists are wrong many, many times in their lives. So if you want to be a good scientist, you have to be willing to be wrong sometimes. And often you learn more when you are wrong because when you find out you're wrong you try to figure out the right explanations.

These are just a few of the many rules of science, but they are the basic ones to help us get started in playing the game. Like many board games that your child plays, there are more "advanced" levels of play for older children. As your child gets older, he or she will learn these advanced rules. Each specific science also has its own special rules; for example, astronomy and biology may have slightly different rules. But all sciences play by the general rules we've just discussed.

Now that we've considered what science is, we'll move on in the next chapter to what science is *not*, and we'll go over some ways to help you and your child tell the difference between things that are scientific and things that are not scientific.

3

Things That Go Bump in the Night: What Science Isn't

In the first chapter I talked about children as natural-born scientists—stimulus seeking, curious, with an innate ability to understand cause-and-effect relationships. While it's true that children are natural scientists in one respect, they need to learn the rules of the game of science, which we discussed in the last chapter. These rules help us to understand not just the cause of things but the *correct* cause of things. But how can we tell the difference between the right causes and the wrong ones? The answer is in knowing the difference between what science is and what science is not. If we play by the rules, we stand a pretty good chance of finding the correct causes of things. In this chapter, we'll look at "things that go bump in the night"—that is, what *isn't* science.

There are a large number of unusual claims made about things like ghosts, monsters, Bigfoot, ESP, reincarnation, the Loch Ness Monster, haunted houses, extraterrestrial beings, and so on. As a kid, I remember being fascinated by some and scared to death of others. I didn't know what to think about these things. It seemed as if science didn't have any answers to help me know whether they were true or not. Everyone talked about monsters and ghosts and such, but no one I knew had ever actually seen one.

How can we find out about these things? What do scientists think about things that go bump in the night? When I was a kid scientists pretty much just didn't think about them. There were no good books *by scientists* about monsters and ghosts. But now things are different. There is now a group called the Committee for the Scientific Investigation of Claims of the Paranormal (CSICOP). This group is a collection of scientists who are skeptics—that is, they try to find natural explanations for unusual claims. There are now dozens of groups loosely affiliated with CSICOP around the world. These groups usually meet on a monthly basis, offering fascinating lectures (open to the public) on a variety of topics, including astrology, psychic phenomena, ESP, ghosts, magic, dowsing, the Bermuda Triangle, reincarnation, UFOs, life after death, faith healing, Bigfoot, the Loch Ness Monster, haunted houses, channeling, firewalking, and so on.

The skeptics only debunk things that turn out not to be valid, which is most of the above. In their presentation their goal is to promote rational and scientific thinking for people of all ages. They frequently have programs for kids, perhaps bringing in professional magicians such as James "The Amazing" Randi to demonstrate how easy it is to trick the eye into believing something that seems impossible. Everyone knows that making an object disappear is just a trick, because the magician *says* that it's a trick and makes no special claims about his ability. But there are other people who don't warn us about their ability to deceive the eye. Instead, they say their ability comes from special powers that the rest of us don't have. Many people believe them. The goal of CSICOP in particular and of scientists in general is to teach people *how* to think, not *what* to think about these special claims. I believe that if children learn how to think scientifically, they will learn not to fear things that go bump in the night.

We may compile a list of things that are not science that would fall into one of two categories: *pseudoscience*, or claims that are not scientific but masquerade as science, and *nonscience*, or claims that are not scientific and make no pretense of being science.

We will be looking at several pseudoscientific claims: monsters, demons, ghosts, and haunted houses; ESP; astrology; and UFOs and extraterrestrial beings. We will then examine two categories of nonscience: myth and religion.

There are certain things to bear in mind when confronting claims of the paranormal. Here are a few questions you might tell your child to ask if he or she hears about any of these ideas at school or from friends:

1. How do you know it's true?
2. Who said it's true?
3. Can you show me that it's true?
4. Is there any scientific evidence that it's true?
5. Is it possible that someone made it up, sort of like Santa Claus, the Easter Bunny, or the tooth fairy?
6. What other ways are there to explain this?
7. Can you do it over and over with the same results?

The reason it is important for your child to understand the differences among science, pseudoscience, and nonscience is threefold. First, there are a lot of hocus-pocus, silly, and just plain foolish claims that people make, and children may be susceptible to believing many of them. These pseudoscientific claims may do no harm to anyone, but why should anyone waste time on them when there is so precious little time to tackle the vast array of scientific questions?

Second, there are many dangerous pseudoscientific claims that can, indeed, do harm to children. Cults often attract individuals by making pseudoscientific claims that appear impressive to the uninitiated, such as the ability to read minds or heal people. Once the cult gets someone in their embraces they utilize a number of brain-washing techniques which, in the end, can lead to drug abuse, illicit sex, and even mass suicide, as in the case of Jim Jones in Guyana. Knowing the difference between science and pseudoscience may literally save your child's life.

Finally, there are many beliefs that are nonscientific and that need not be threatened by science. Myths and religions are two we shall discuss. Now let's take a look at some of these claims and see what science has to say about them.

PSEUDOSCIENCE

Monsters and Demons, Ghosts and Haunted Houses

This is a particularly important category for young children, because it is not unusual for them to have bad dreams about creatures or monsters or to have heard stories about ghosts and haunted houses. And there are so many movies, television shows, and cartoons that have monsters and ghosts in them that it isn't surprising that children are interested or concerned.

For all the claims made and tests conducted to discover any evidence for the existence of monsters and ghosts, none has ever been validated. There is *no* hard evidence for the existence of such beasties as the Loch Ness Monster, Bigfoot, living dinosaurs, unicorns, fairies, or demons of any kind. The so-called "hard" evidence presented by people usually consists of very grainy photographs, blurred images, or some trick photography. But when analyzed by scientists and experts in photography, all of these claims have been either refuted or shown to lack enough evidence for a decision to be made one way or the other about whether the thing really exists or not. For a complete analysis of all these claims see the following books, as noted in the bibliography in Appendix 1: Martin Gardner's *Science: Good, Bad and Bogus*, George Abell and Barry Singer's *Science and the Paranormal*, and James Randi's *Flim-Flam!*

Extrasensory Perception (ESP)

If something is *extrasensory*, by definition it can't be sensed. People who claim to have ESP frequently pretend they are being scientific. They claim to have a "sixth sense" or a "mysterious force" that crosses the barrier of space between two individuals, allowing them to "read minds."

We can test ESP scientifically, and James Randi and the skeptics in CSICOP have done so many times. The individuals claiming such powers have *never* succeeded in passing the scientific test. They have failed every time. And when "parapsychologists" who purport to study ESP scientifically have been investigated by other scientists, their scientific methods have been shown to leave much to be desired.

But let's not just criticize; let's do an experiment. You and your child can test each other's ESP right now. Get a deck of cards and take the four aces from a deck: the ace of spades, the ace of hearts, the ace of clubs, and the ace of diamonds. You be the person taking the test. You will read the backs of the playing cards as your child marks an *X* or an *O* for a "hit" or a "miss." Give the four cards to your child and have her mix them up and put them face down. Next, she should hold the cards up, one at a time, so that the back of the card is facing you. You guess, or "sense," what the card is and state so verbally. Your child then marks either *X* or *O* on a piece of paper, without telling you which card was chosen. After you've gone through the four cards she can mix them up and try again. We'll call this set a "trial." Go through a lot of trials—let's say ten in all, so you will have had a total of forty guesses.

By chance or luck alone you should get one out of four correct, just by guessing. If you do forty guesses, you should get ten *X*'s and thirty *O*'s. It's likely you won't get these *exact* figures, but they should be close. (This is also a good way to teach your child a little math: By chance alone you or your child should get one-fourth, or 25 percent, correct. The probability of getting a "hit" is therefore 25 percent.)

Now switch places with your child, and let her try to "sense" what cards you hold up. Her results will be similar to yours, though the exact figures will vary.

Your results will have proved scientifically that neither you nor your child has ESP. This experiment, by the way, does *not* prove that ESP doesn't exist; it just proves that under these conditions ESP was not found.

What the scientific method does is filter out real claims from others. Most important, science can teach a child to be skeptical of unusual claims rather than accepting them at face value, no matter how real they may seem.

Astrology

Astrology is the belief that the alignment of the moon, sun, planets, and stars at the time of your birth shapes and controls your personality and destiny. Astrology is pseudoscience because astrologers like to pretend that what they are doing is scientific.

The similarity between the words *astrology* and *astronomy* often confuses people. Also, many centuries ago astrology and astronomy were one and the same profession. Astrologers studied the stars in order to understand and predict things that were happening on earth. But since then astronomy has become science, and astrology has remained what it was back then—superstition.

Astrology is wrong for a variety of reasons, two of which I'll mention. One is that the moon, sun, planets, and stars have very little gravitational effect on us. For example, you can hold this book up to your child and tell him it has as much gravitational influence on him as Mars! Second, at the present time the so-called "signs of the zodiac" are all off by one sign because of the fact that the earth wobbles like a top, and the North Pole therefore "points" to different constellations than it did back when the original astrological charts were devised, thousands of years ago.

So why is astrology so popular? Because to many people, it seems to work. How does it work? There are several possibilities. One, the astrologer may make broad, sweeping predictions that could fit almost anyone, such as: "You will encounter some difficulty at the end of the month." Or: "I see a cloud over the White House in December." What kind of predictions are these? Almost anything that happens will fit.

Two, the astrologer will make a prediction that is certain to come true. "There will be a major earthquake in California," is an example. What does "major" mean? There are earthquakes all the time in California. Which one was the "major" one?

Three, the astrologer will generally describe your personality in a glowing light: "You're very intelligent and insightful. You understand people and have a good sense of humor." Well, who doesn't think of themselves as intelligent and insightful? Who doesn't feel they understand people and have a good sense of humor? That's a pretty safe description.

Four, if astrologers make specific predictions, they make so many of them that some are bound to come true. We just forget the rest. Every January 1 astrologers make predictions about the coming year which usually include the lives of politicians, movie stars, and other notables. If they make enough predictions about election results and movie star divorces, they are bound to be right a few times. It's these hits that we are reminded about, not the misses.

Astrology is really a form of entertainment, not a science of reading people's personalities or predicting human fortunes and misfortunes.

UFOs and Extraterrestrials

This is a favorite form of pseudoscience among children and adults alike. Fueled by such blockbuster movies as *E.T.* and *Close Encounters of the Third Kind*, children's imaginations have run wild. But even if you tell your child that "it's just a movie," there is no lack of books about UFOs claiming that extraterrestrials are not science fiction but science *fact*. One study showed that one out of five Americans believes that aliens have landed on earth.

As far as we know aliens have not landed on earth. Or if they have, they never seem to be seen by scientists. And if there is any reputable scientist who would love to find extraterrestrial intelligent life forms, it's the famous astronomer Carl Sagan. Sagan has written at length about the possibilities of extraterrestrial life, including a best-selling science-fiction novel, *Contact*. He had an entire episode on the subject in his famed "Cosmos" television series. Sagan has even spearheaded project SETI (Search for Extraterrestrial Intelligence). Sagan is probably as knowledgeable as anyone in the world about whether there is life beyond the earth, and he claims that there isn't one shred of evidence for the existence of UFOs or extraterrestrials. As scientists, we must conclude that we simply don't know if there is life elsewhere.

But let's not just take Sagan's word for it. After all, Rule 3 in the game of science is to challenge authority and check things for yourself, right? We already know from many unmanned space flights that there appears to be no other life in our solar system, so any extraterrestrials would have to come from other star systems. If you were to do an experiment holding a beach ball to represent the sun, with your child holding another beach ball to represent the closest star to our sun, he would have to stand about 2,000 miles away! The closest star to our sun is billions of miles away. It would take our fastest rocket tens of thousands of years to get there. Impossible! And that's the *closest* star—most are much farther away. The chances of aliens having managed to find our minuscule little planet in a vast ocean of empty space is stretching the imagination of even the wildest science-fiction writers.

The nineteenth-century biologist Thomas Huxley once noted: "The more a statement of fact conflicts with previous experience, the more complete must be the evidence which is to justify us in believing it." In short, says Marcello Truzzi, "extraordinary claims demand extraordinary evidence." As exciting as it would be to have extraordinary evidence for UFOs and extraterrestrials, we don't have *any* evidence yet.

NONSCIENCE

Myths

The late Joseph Campbell, the world's foremost authority on myths, said that myths give us a way to understand meaning in the world. But this meaning is not the kind that science provides, which is an understanding of *how* things work. Myths provide thoughts on the meaning of *why* things are—the meaning of life, the reason for living, the basis of love, the value of marriage, the love of heroes, and that sort of thing, all from a human point of view. According to Campbell, we are all looking for "an experience of being alive, so that our life experiences . . . will have resonances within our own innermost being and reality, so that we actually feel the rapture of being alive." In other words, while myths make living more fun, this doesn't make them true.

For example, take every child's favorite science-fiction story: *Star Wars*. *Star Wars* is a myth about heroes and villains, good guys and bad guys, and about having the courage to face evil and take the risk to help other people, which makes you a better person. Myths are great for kids, because they usually teach some moral lesson about striving to be your best and helping other people.

Myths don't even have to be "science"-fiction stories. When I was a boy I read about the exploits of Don Quixote in his pursuit of "the impossible dream." He fought against villains, saved damsels in distress, jousted against a windmill, and helped other people. But *Don Quixote* is the same myth as *Star Wars*, with different heroes and villains. It's good for children to have heroes, and myths provide bigger-than-life heroes.

Myths, however, are not scientific. These things don't really exist anywhere. They're just fun and exciting and provide your child with role models for good behavior. Science is fun and exciting too, but in a different way, and it does have at least one moral lesson that would be wonderful for all children to learn. If you recall, Rule 6 of science is that disputes are settled with evidence, not with insults and attacks. Science waits for the evidence to come in before making decisions and, preferably, remains nonjudgmental. Everyone knows what prejudice is—it's the *pre*judging of someone or something based on insufficient evidence or irrelevent criteria, such as skin color or religion. Science doesn't use prejudice. Rather, it uses *"postjudice"*—that is, it *post*judges someone, after having given them a fair chance. Science provides children, and everyone else, with this moral lesson.

But, in general, science doesn't give us purpose in life; myths and religions do. Science doesn't tell us "what it all means." Nature doesn't give us moral messages—nature is what it is, regardless of what we *think* it is. This is why religion and myths are so important to people. Science, as powerful as it is, should not be looked to for these final answers. It's okay to tell your child about myths (preferably the good ones). Just make sure that he or she knows these are not part of science.

Religion

What does science have to say about God? In a word, *nothing*. God is not something that can be tested in an experiment, and different religious beliefs cannot be clarified through the scientific method. Religion and God are *nonscientific* ideas, though far too many people think that you have to be either religious *or* scientific, but not both. I frequently run into this fallacy among students in my evolution class. Many of them worry that if they believe in evolution they will have to give up their religion or won't be able to believe in God at all. Nothing could be further from the truth. There are many, many scientists who are practicing Jews, Christians, Muslims, or whatever. There are also plenty who are agnostics—that is, they are either not sure whether there is a God or not, or they don't think it's possible to ever know for sure, so they don't take sides.

The point is that science and religion are two completely different ways of searching for truth, but they are not mutually exclusive. If they were, then those scientists who are religious would be inconsistent, and I don't think they are. It's okay to be both religious and scientific.

What science does do in this regard is make it possible to reject "false gods," such as those that aboriginal societies attach to such things as lightning. The Roman thinker Polybius once said, "Whenever it is possible to find out the cause of what is happening, one should not have recourse to the gods." By this he meant gods of nature, not the Christian God. Science does not remove the possibility of God. It just makes it possible to understand the world without having to resort to the type of gods referred to by Polybius.

Science has its place and its limits. It's great for some things, and useless for others. The key is in understanding the difference. As *Astronomy* magazine columnist Rick Shaffer has noted: "There are aspects of the human condition or experience that are not subject to the scientific method, mostly because they are not reproducible. Individuals may have real experiences which are truly inexplicable, but since they cannot be reproduced, science has nothing to say about them." We live in a rich world filled with science and nonscience, and no one has a monopoly on the truth. Science, for example, does not tell us right from wrong, moral from immoral, good from bad. Teaching your child science does not mean teaching him to be good or bad. Science does not tell us how to behave, nor can it help us judge the value of something. Whether Mozart was better than the Beatles is not a question that scientists could ever answer. That's not to say that scientists don't have opinions on these matters—they most definitely do—but their opinions are not scientific ones. As Stephen Jay Gould once remarked,

> Science teaches us many wonderful and disturbing things—facts that need weighing when we try to develop standards of conduct and ponder the great questions of morals and aesthetics. But science cannot dictate social policy. We live with poets and politicians, preachers and philosophers. All have their ways of knowing, and all are valid in their proper domains. The world is too complex and interesting for one way to have all the answers.

What I have attempted to do in this chapter has been to show the importance of understanding the differences among science, pseudoscience, and nonscience, and why these distinctions are important. Carl Sagan once said that "if science were presented to the public in an interesting way, there would be no room for pseudoscience." I agree—and that, in a nutshell, is one of the goals of this book. So now that we've completed the first section, on getting excited about science, let's *do* some science!

PART TWO

Doing Science

"We may wallow forever in the thinkable;
science traffics in the doable."

STEPHEN JAY GOULD

CHAPTER

4

How Science Is Done

Now that we have some understanding of what science is, let's take a look at how science is done. In the next chapter we will do dozens of scientific experiments. The experiments may all differ in detail, but they have certain common characteristics. These characteristics form the basis of the *scientific method*, which will be discussed in this chapter.

A technical definition of the scientific method that is satisfactory to all scholars and scientists is almost impossible to devise. This is probably why there are so many scholarly books that cover this very subject. Suffice it to say that the scientific method is a key issue in science. We might summarize the scientific method in the following simple four-step process, which we will be using in our experiments. In reality science is not this simple or linear. But this outline gives us a framework from which to begin to understand how science in done.

THE SCIENTIFIC METHOD

Step 1: Observation

The first thing a scientist does is gather information about the world around her. She tries to learn as much as possible about a subject by both reading in libraries and observing in nature. It is important that a scientist not *start* with a conclusion and then look for things to support what she already believes. That is the way pseudoscientists work.

To your child:

The first step in the scientific method is what scientists call *observation*. It means they look around the world and see everything they can see, and get as much information as possible so that they can do good experiments. Scientists try not to look just for things they are hoping to find, because then they might miss something else they weren't looking for.

Step 2: Generalization

The next step is to make a generalization (which scientists call a "hypothesis") about the specific observations you have made. Such a generalization is also known informally as a "testable guess," or a conclusion that best explains what has been observed.

To your child:

After a scientist has gathered up a whole bunch of facts about the world, he then tries to see what it all means. It's sort of like putting a puzzle together. After you have a lot of pieces you might be able to see what the big picture looks like. When the scientist makes a generalization after gathering observations, it's like guessing what a puzzle is by looking at a lot of the pieces.

Step 3: Prediction

Once you've made a generalization to try to explain your observations, the next step is to make a prediction based on that generalization. A prediction is a statement that should follow, if the generalization is true.

To your child:

A prediction is something a scientist does after she has gathered information and made some guesses as to what the pieces of information mean. Once the scientist has made a guess as to what the pieces of the puzzle will look like when they are put together, she then makes a prediction. For instance, she might say, "I think the puzzle is a picture of a horse. If I check the box cover of the puzzle, I think it will show a picture of a horse."

Step 4: Experimentation

To determine whether a prediction is true, the scientist must do an experiment to verify or reject the generalization. These experiments, like the ones we'll do in the next chapter, form the backbone of science. What this means, of course, is that in order for something to be scientific, it must be falsifiable—that is, you have to be able to disprove it. If you try to disprove it but can't, this makes you that much more confident in your prediction.

To your child:

If a scientist makes a prediction, he is really excited about checking whether he was right or not. Do you know how scientists check their predictions? They do experiments. We're going to do some experiments in a minute to see how they work. An experiment will either disprove or support a scientific idea.

THE SCIENTIFIC METHOD IN ACTION

You and your child can do a simple experiment to see how this four-step process works. Go to a place where there are a lot of people—maybe a park or a supermarket—and *observe* that nearly everyone with long hair is a female and that nearly everyone with short hair is a male. After you've observed lots of people, you might make a *generalization,* or hypothesis, that females tend to have long hair and males tend to have short hair. To take your generalization further, make a *prediction* that everywhere you go females will tend to have long hair and males will tend to have short hair. To test your prediction, do an *experiment.* Go to other places where people are, and see if the females tend to have long hair and the males tend to have short hair. If they do, then your generalization has been verified by your experiment.

Let's look at another example of the scientific method in action, but this time it's one in which the experiment *won't* verify the generalization. This is an experiment with a twist. Your child comes home one day after riding his bicycle and complains that it isn't working very well—it's harder than usual for him to pedal it, because the wheels don't seem to turn very easily. As an observant scientist, you record your child's comments and descriptions in the first step, *observation*. Next, you make a *generalization* about his comments, forming the hypothesis that the wheels are rubbing against the brakes. In step three, you make the *prediction* that if this is true, one or both of the brakes will be pushed up against the rim of the wheel. Step four is to conduct an *experiment* to verify your generalization: You look down at the wheels to see whether the brakes are touching them. Maybe you even spin them around to see if they are hitting. You find that they are not rubbing. In this case, the experiment does *not* verify the generalization, which means that your generalization was wrong. Now, you do what any good scientist would do—you go back to step two, and form a new generalization: The bike has a flat tire. In step three, you make the prediction that if this is true, then one of the tires will be "squishy" or "soft" to the touch. In step four, you conduct an experiment to verify your prediction: you push down on the front tire. It's hard, so you do a second experiment, pushing down on the back tire. It's squishy, which tells you that the back tire is flat and verifies your generalization.

You have successfully solved the problem, and you have done so scientifically! In a way, doing science is just like solving the problems that we all do in daily life. Scientists just do it a bit more formally and carefully. As Thomas Huxley said, "Science is simply common sense at its best—that is, rigidly accurate in observation, and merciless to fallacy in logic."

These examples, of course, are simplified for clarification of the basic framework of science. When you're actually in a laboratory doing science the "steps" will not be so obvious because they are going on inside the scientist's mind. And since science is a human endeavor, there are human emotions involved. As Paul MacCready notes, "Science progresses in a nonlinear fashion. There are hunches, false starts, emotions, idea exchanges, and what looks like a lot of randomness. In the end experiments will verify or reject these ideas, but the process of getting there is quite dynamic and very exciting."

LET'S FORM A THEORY

Now that we have a generalization (or hypothesis) that has been verified by experiment, what do we do? If the generalization has been tested many times by many scientists and has always seemed to hold true, then the scientist might develop a *theory*. A theory is a well-supported generalization that tries to describe the observations and make predictions. Stephen Hawking says that a theory is a "good theory if it satisfies two requirements: It must accurately describe a large class of observations on the basis of a model that contains only a few arbitrary elements, and it must make definite predictions about the results of future observations." For instance, in the example used earlier, you might develop a theory that all females have long hair and all males have short hair because long hair is like other characteristics that make females different from males—they're just born that way. If this theory were true, then *all* males would have short hair, with no exceptions. But the theory is false, because not all males have short hair. In fact, as we saw in the 1960s and 1970s (and still do today, somewhat), there are plenty of males who do grow their hair just as long as females do. So we must develop another theory that says that the reason most females have long hair and most males have short hair is social customs, not biological constraints. This would be a more reasonable theory, one that is based on the *facts*.

WHAT ARE FACTS?

Facts are the "things" we see, hear, smell, touch, and taste in the world around us. Facts are what we observe in step one of the scientific method. As one philosopher of science said, "Facts are the world's data." They are the things that give us clues to solving nature's puzzles.

But some people are confused by the word *fact*. They think it means something that is known with 100 percent certainty. You've probably heard someone say, "That's a fact. I know it for sure" or "It's not a fact; it's just a theory." This makes us think that somehow a theory is not as good as a fact, and that a fact is something we know "for sure." As we saw in the rules of the game in chapter 2, however, nothing is certain in science. There are no facts in science, if by facts we mean things that have been proved with 100 percent certainty. There *are* facts, if we mean the things of the world we can study. As the Russian physiologist Ivan Pavlov said, "Facts are the air of scientists. Without them, you never can fly."

For instance, consider the following statement: It is currently 76 degrees Fahrenheit outside. This is a fact, in the sense that temperature is part of the world's data. You can go outside and look at a thermometer and observe this fact of nature. You could *not* say, however, that you know with 100 percent certainty that it is 76 degrees Fahrenheit outside—the thermometer may be off a little, or perhaps you haven't read it exactly right, or maybe the glass in the thermometer is cracked, changing the pressure on the mercury and giving a skewed reading, and so on.

All the experiments in the next chapter will reveal the facts of the world to us, but we should always remember that no matter how many experiments we do, nothing will ever be known for certain. That's the exciting part about science.

GUIDELINES FOR DOING SCIENCE WITH YOUR CHILD

It doesn't take a lot to do science. In fact, it takes a lot less than most of us might think. In the book *To Know a Fly*, the biologist Vincent Dethier outlines what most of us think are the necessary ingredients for doing science: "a college education, a substantial grant from the federal government, a secretary, a research associate, two laboratory assistants, permanent equipment, consumable supplies, travel, a station wagon for field collecting, photographic supplies, books, animals, animal cages, somebody to care for the animals, postage, telephone calls . . . " No wonder so many people are afraid of science! But Dethier quickly dispels this myth, and tells us what a scientist (in this case, a biologist) really needs: "Anyone with a genuine love of nature, an insatiable curiosity about life, a soaring imagination, devilish ingenuity, the patience of Job, and the ability to read has the basic ingredients and most of the necessary accoutrements to become a first-class biologist." And virtually every child has these ingredients. In other words, doing science can cost practically nothing. All you need is the desire.

Here are a few guidelines for you to follow when doing science with your child:

1.   **AS WITH THE SCIENTIFIC METHOD, BEGIN WITH OBSERVATIONS, BOTH IN BOOKS AND IN NATURE.**

One great place to begin to help your child formulate observations about the world is the library. Science books will help both of you to learn what to look for when you go outside to study nature. I remember taking a vacation with my parents when I was a boy in which we drove across the California desert and into the mountains of Arizona. I mostly read books during the drive, because just looking at pretty mountains was boring to me. Years later, after having studied geology, taking that same drive seemed completely different to me. It was as if I had never been there before! Now I was studying the rock formations and the geological strata intensely, and looking at different mountains as examples of different theories of mountain formation that I had read about.

Carl Sagan recalls that his intense quest for scientific knowledge began when his parents gave him a library card. Sagan immediately headed for the library to check out a book so that he might understand what the bright lights in the night sky were. "I would ask older children and adults, who would only reply, 'They're lights in the sky, kid.' I could *see* they were lights in the sky. But what *were* they?" A youthful Sagan asked the librarian for a book on stars:

> She returned with a picture book displaying portraits of men and women with names like Clark Gable and Jean Harlow. I complained, and for some reason then obscure to me, she smiled and found another book—the right kind of book. I opened it breathlessly and read until I found it. The book said something astonishing, a very big thought. It said that the stars were suns, only very far away. The Sun was a star, but close up. So I decided that I would be an astronomer, learn about the stars and planets and, if I could, go and visit them.

2.   TELL YOUR CHILD THAT THERE ARE NO DUMB QUESTIONS.

In a book on the psychology of solving problems, psychologists discovered that in many ways children are actually better problem solvers than adults, because they are more willing to admit mistakes, give up wrong ideas, and continue asking questions, smart or dumb, until they get the right answers. These psychologists found that adults are far more anxious about being "wrong," and therefore become afraid to ask "dumb" questions.

Scientists are like children in this respect. Sagan, in fact, credits his success as an adult scientist to the influencing factors in his childhood: "It has been my immense good fortune to have parents and some teachers who encouraged this odd ambition." Sagan stresses the importance of trying to answer children's questions about the world around them properly. Answers such as "They're lights in the sky, kid" are inadequate for the insatiably curious (children and scientists). As Sagan notes:

> Every time I talk to first-graders, I get such a lift because they are clearly natural-born scientists. They don't know what constitutes a dumb question yet. So they are able to ask all the deep questions unself-consciously. Later on, they are taught that those are dumb questions. For example, Why is the sun round? Why is grass green?—and those types of questions. Unfortunately, there are many adults whose answer is something like: "What did you expect the sun to be—*square?*" Then the kid gets a sense that there is something reprehensible about this kind of question, and after asking a few of them and getting this response figures, "Okay, I'd better not ask these kinds of questions anymore," and we've lost another mind.

3. EXPLAIN SCIENCE IN WORDS CHILDREN CAN UNDERSTAND.

One of the primary goals of this book is to help parents not only understand science, but to also be able to put the language of science into words and concepts that children can understand. I suspect that one of the reasons for this adult response to children's "dumb" questions is that adults either don't know the answers or don't know how to put them into language a child can understand. For example, a complete and scientifically accurate answer to a simple question like why the sun is round is clearly not appropriate. As Sagan warns:

> [Saying that] "The sun is round because gravity is a central force and the tension and yield strength of the sun are not enough to hold up departures from symmetry" is probably not the right answer for a five-year-old. But you *could* say, "It's round because gravity pulls everything in equally." Or, "Gee, what an interesting question. And the moon is round, and the other planets are round. There must be something that is making them round. Let's try to look it up in the encyclopedia." Or, "Beats me, kid. Maybe nobody knows. Maybe when you grow up you'll be the first to find out."

In other words, whenever possible try to find out the answer to a child's question by looking it up. If you can't find the answer, or there is no answer, try to leave the child with a note of optimism—if no one knows, maybe she'll be the first to make the discovery. This is the sort of situation of which dreams are made.

4. LOOK IT UP BEFORE YOU LEAP.

To explain a principle of science to your child, you must first understand it yourself. This requires a little effort on your part, but the rewards are well worth it. Not only will your child then be better able to understand the principle, but you yourself will have learned something new. On top of that, this communication will give you an opportunity to grow closer to your child in a new and different way.

The seven appendices at the end of this book are themselves a sourcebook for looking things up and following through with science activities. One of the (tongue-in-cheek) rules for first-year science teachers is to stay one chapter ahead of the students. The same rule applies to parents. Take a few minutes to read in the encyclopedia or other science books about what science you and your child are about to do. This will not only make the experience more rewarding for your child, but it will also make you look good!

5. ENCOURAGE EXCELLENCE AND BOLDNESS.

When I reflect on my own childhood, none of the *traditional* environmental conditions was present to lead me to develop a passion for the sciences. My parents were not scientists; neither were my older brothers and sisters, nor any other of my relatives. I therefore had no scientific role models in my immediate sphere of influence. In fact, my folks were not even college educated. Yet they provided two subtle, but key ingredients that shaped a curious and productive personality in me: a desire to pursue excellence in whatever I undertook, and the boldness to try almost anything, as long as I did it with excellence. They bought me books, rewarded me for reading by giving me other things that I liked (such as model kits), bought an encyclopedia set (which I frequently leafed through for hours in a rather haphazard fashion, reading whatever sections grabbed my attention), gave me lessons in whatever it was that I wanted to learn (and a couple of things I had no interest in learning!), and generally encouraged me to be brave enough to try new things. I was almost never restricted, and I think such leniency (within certain bounds) leads to greater courage in the face of the unknown. And a scientist faces the unknown almost every day. In fact, it is the business of science to confront the unknown. As the atomic scientist J. Robert Oppenheimer observed, "There must be no barriers to freedom of inquiry. The scientist is free, and must be free to ask any question, to doubt any assertion, to seek for any evidence, to correct any errors."

6. IT'S OKAY TO SAY "I DON'T KNOW."

This is probably the most important guideline of those discussed here. When trying to explain scientific concepts to others, the tendency is to fill in partial knowledge as complete knowledge. But, as they say, a little knowledge can be dangerous. It's dangerous because it lulls you into thinking you know enough to answer a question properly, when you actually don't. As a college professor I encounter this quite frequently in myself! When students ask questions that I am not really equipped to answer properly, I usually have *some* clue as to what the answer might be, but I'm not really sure. So I attempt the ubiquitous "educated guess." This can be a mistake for both teachers and parents, because the educated guess is wrong at least as frequently as it is right.

The best answer to a question you don't know much about is "I don't know." From there you can look it up, or have your child look it up, or, better still, you and your child can look it up together. It's difficult for us to say "I don't know," because we want to appear knowledgeable; it feels good to "know," and maybe it feels a little bad to appear ignorant. But it's a dangerous practice to feign knowledge, because you may be wrong. As British television-documentary producer James Burke ("Connections" and "The Day the Universe Changed") says, "Certainty is a kind of prison. When you are absolutely certain, you are also possibly absolutely blind."

In addition, saying "I don't know" to your child teaches him that it's okay for him to confess ignorance to something he may not know much about. Your willingness to admit a lack of knowledge will also teach your child about the very core of science: We must wait for sufficient evidence before drawing a conclusion. Scientists collect a mass of facts and data before cautiously putting forth a generalization, or hypothesis. And only after many experiments have confirmed and verified that generalization do they just as cautiously put forward a theory to explain all the data. The pseudoscientist, on the other hand, jumps quickly to conclusions, usually with inadequate or no data, and tells everyone he has the answer. As Sagan says, "It's all right to reserve judgment until the evidence is in."

Teaching children to say "I don't know" in science also teaches them to say "I don't know" to other problems in life. They learn to wait for more evidence before drawing a conclusion—in other words, they learn to practice "postjudice" instead of prejudice. As in our democratic society, where the judicial system says a person is innocent until proved guilty, wouldn't it be great if we practiced the same philosophy individually in judging other people? The great astronomer and physicist Sir Arthur Stanley Eddington said, "Observation is the supreme court of appeal." As children learn the scientific method, it's just possible that they will develop their own "judicial systems" and will be willing to reserve judgment until the evidence is in, not only in science, but in other spheres of human interaction as well.

BUILDING A SCIENCE

The way science is done is similar, in a way, to how a building is built. The facts of the world, and the observations and generalizations made about those facts (the first two steps of the scientific method) are like the stone and mortar of a building. But as the French physicist Henri Poincaré once said, "A group of facts is no more a science than a pile of bricks is a building." To build a building, or a science, we need blueprints. Predictions, experiments, and theories form the blueprints of science.

Rome wasn't built in a day, and neither is the edifice of science. It takes a long time to build a science. Years, even decades, of cataloging observations, forming generalizations, making predictions, and conducting experiments all lead to theories, forming the blueprints of a science. In the next chapter we will do dozens of experiments that reveal, by way of example, how the scientific method comes alive, and how the accumulated findings of experiments build a science into a universally valid body of knowledge. In addition, you and your child are going to build the experience of doing science the way scientists do.

CHAPTER
5

3-D Science:
Science You Can
Do at Home

Let's start this chapter off with a question: Do you know why it's warmer in the summer and cooler in the winter? If you answered that this is because the earth is closer to the sun in the summer and farther away in the winter, you would be in agreement with many Harvard University graduates of the class of 1988. You'd also be dead wrong. The earth is actually closest to the sun in January! The different warming and cooling periods—the seasons—are caused by the tilt of the earth's axis in relation to its orbit. On one side of the orbit, we (in the United States) are positioned on the earth in such a way that the sun is directly overhead at noon, which makes it hotter. This is summer. When we are on the other side of the orbit, the sun is low in the sky at noon, and the daylight period is shorter, so it is cooler. This is winter. The opposite is true for countries in the southern hemisphere, such as Australia. This is why they have their summer during our winter.

Harvard University astrophysicist Irwin Shapiro, who conducted this brief survey of Harvard seniors, is distressed at the lack of understanding of such basic principles of science. So he started a method known as STAR, which stands for "Science Teaching through its Astronomical Roots." Shapiro's method is based on the philosophy that "it's impossible to understand an astronomy diagram without using three dimensions." The importance of the three-dimensional, hands-on approach to science cannot be overstressed. It's one thing to describe a scientific phenomenon in words, as I did above. It's quite another to see a model of it in action. As Shapiro says: "High-school science textbooks are impossible. They are dense with concepts and jargon. No one understands what's going on." Later in this chapter, for example, we'll *see* why there are seasons, instead of just *saying* why.

This chapter is on 3-D science, or science you can do at home with your child so that he or she can actually *see* and *do* science rather than just reading about it. If it works for college students (those using Shapiro's STAR method do about 30 percent better than ordinary students), it will work even better with children, who *need* visual demonstrations not only to explain complex concepts but also to hold their attention. We will perform simple and fun experiments that can be done at home using inexpensive materials.

Since science is an attempt to answer questions about nature, in this chapter I have posed thirty-six questions, each of which we will try to answer with a simple experiment. Experiments are like a library card to nature, allowing you to explore nature's knowledge. Sample experiments will be set up for each of the following sciences: physics, astronomy, chemistry, biology, earth sciences, and psychology. I have chosen these as the major demarcations among fields of thought in the sciences. Naturally, there are many subdisciplines within each of these categories, and you can learn more about these by first examining Appendix 7, *Mapping the Sciences*, and then going to Appendices 1, 2, and 3 for references on other books and magazines for these specific disciplines.

Following each experimental question is a brief background to the experiment, a list of the required materials, directions for the parent, and where appropriate, a "To Your Child" section. Some of the experiments are accompanied by an illustration. I recommend reading through the entire experiment first to familiarize yourself, set up the materials, and then bring your child into the activity. I have conducted all of these experiments myself with children and found that a little over an hour is about the maximum time limit of a seven-year-old's attention span for science experiments. In general I have found, especially with boys, that the more "things" there are to do, and the more "bang for the buck" in the experiment, the longer their attention is held. Boys seem to love matches, fire, and burning things! Naturally not all science experiments can involve these activities, so it's best to mix them up a bit. Certainly you don't need to follow the order in which I have presented these experiments.

PHYSICS

Physics is the study of matter and energy and how these interact in certain fields of study, including the studies of light, sound, heat, and energy. I offer you and your child nine experiments through which you can demonstrate these different subjects.

Light

1.   WHAT COLOR IS LIGHT?

To parents: Ever since the Renaissance, people have been doing experiments to figure out what makes up light. It was Newton who first figured out that white light *isn't* white. He discovered this by doing the experiment you and your child will do now. You will find out what white light is made of by passing it through a special device that separates it into its component parts. This device is called a prism, which you can get at most toy stores or hobby shops.

Materials

A prism
A piece of white paper
Sunlight

Directions: Position the prism so that sunlight passes through it, holding the piece of white paper behind it so that the colors can be cast upon the paper (Figure 1). This is called "refraction," which is the bending of light by another material—in this case, the glass of the prism. When Newton did this almost 300 years ago, the sunlight was broken down into the colors of the rainbow. As it turns out, white light is not an entity in itself but a combination of many individual colors. Newton also did the opposite experiment, passing the colors of the rainbow through a prism—

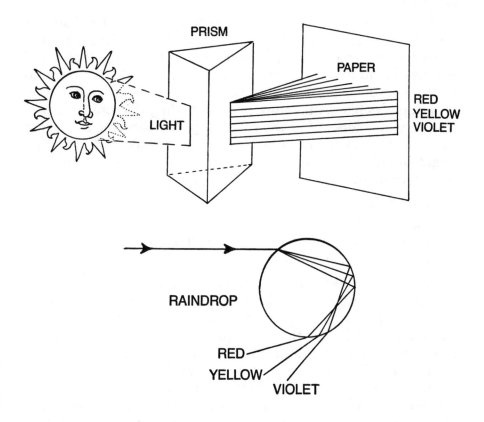

FIGURE 1

and out came white light! You can do this, too, using a second prism. Newton later wrote a very famous book, *Optics*, based on these experiments.

To your child:

If we want to understand how a watch works, we take it apart. We can do the same with light. To understand how light works, we take it apart. This [showing the prism] is called a prism. When you pass white light through it watch what happens. [Do the experiment.]

White light is actually a whole bunch of colors—the colors of the rainbow.

2. WHAT IS A RAINBOW?

To parents: I remember, as a kid, playing with a prism like that used in the experiment above, and seeing that sunlight is broken down into the colors of the rainbow. I then wondered if this had any relation to the rainbows we see after a rain. By looking it up in the encyclopedia, I discovered that, sure enough, each tiny raindrop acts like a miniature prism, dividing the sun's light into a variety of colors. All of the colors together combine to make a rainbow. A raindrop acts just like a prism, breaking down white light (sunlight) into a variety of colors. Millions of raindrops produce a rainbow.

Materials

Sunlight
A spherical or rounded glass jar to fill with water
A rainbow (if available!)

Directions: You can do this yourself at home by filling a spherical jar with water and taking it outside to let the sun shine through it. If you hold it just right, with a piece of white paper (or concrete) behind it for the colors to shine on, you should see the same effect you saw with the prism: a "rainbow" of colors.

You can also try creating your own rainbow with a sprinkler system or "rainbird." If the water is sprayed high and in a fine enough mist, you might see a rainbow develop. You will probably have to walk around the mist in order to find the right position.

Interestingly, one of the first scientific experiments ever made in the Middle Ages was by a German monk named Theodoric, who in 1310 passed sunlight through a sphere of water (as you just did) and got the colors of the rainbow on a sheet of white paper behind it. He had also looked closely through a dewdrop on a plant in the early morning and had seen the same effect. (Try this one as well with your child. One morning when it is a bit cool and there is dew on the plants and flowers in the yard, put your eye right up to a dewdrop, with the sun behind it—being careful not to look directly into the sun—and you will notice that the colors of the rainbow appear in the tiny drop of water!) Theodoric reasoned that each raindrop refracts the light (like a prism) into a different color, and that depending on where you stand, the raindrops across the sky would all refract different colors, giving the rainbow effect. For further details on different types of rainbows and their causes, see Robert Greenler's book *Rainbows, Halos, and Glories*, cited in Appendix 1.

To your child:

Do you remember seeing a rainbow on a rainy day? A rainbow is caused by each raindrop's acting like a tiny prism, just as in the experiment we did with the prism. To see how this works, we'll fill up this glass jar and pretend it's a giant raindrop. See how the "raindrop" creates a rainbow of colors? Millions of raindrops in the clouds form a rainbow when the sun is coming out right after it rains.

3.   HOW DOES A TELESCOPE WORK?

To parents: As a boy I first learned about lenses and telescopes by playing with a simple magnifying glass. I would hold it up to the sun and focus the sun's rays onto a piece of paper, which quickly caught fire.

There are three things to be learned from this kind of experiment. First of all, it demonstrates the power of the sun in a very dramatic way.

Second, it shows that the magnifying glass works in a manner similar to the prism—it refracts light. Instead of refracting it into colors, however, it refracts or bends it all into a point, called the *focal point* (see Figure 2).

Third, a magnifying glass also demonstrates how a telescope works. A magnifying glass is a lens of sorts, and like most lenses, it bends light into a point. A telescope is basically a light-gathering device, too. The bigger the telescope, the greater its ability to gather light. A simple refracting telescope gathers light just like a magnifying glass, but it includes an eyepiece at the focal point to magnify the tiny image for your eye to see. (WARNING: For this reason, as in the example above with the magnifying glass and the sun, you should *never* point a telescope at the sun. If you looked into the eyepiece when the telescope was pointed at the sun, the retina in your eye would immediately be burned, and you would be blinded for life. To look at a solar eclipse, you need to put a "solar filter" over the lens or eyepiece that blocks out 99.999 percent of the sun's light. Use only an approved solar filter that also blocks infrared and ultraviolet light.)

There are actually two types of telescopes: *refracting*, as described above, and *reflecting*. In a reflecting telescope, a mirror is

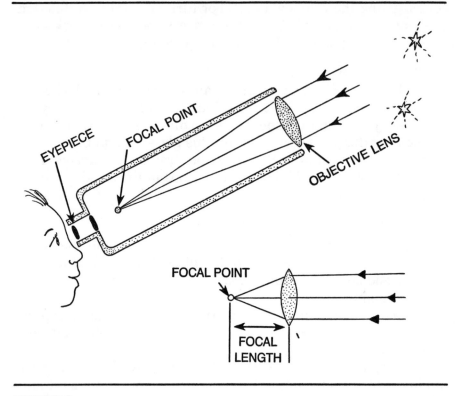

FIGURE 2

used instead of a lens to bring the light rays to a focal point, where an eyepiece then magnifies them for you to see. With a refracting telescope that can be purchased at toy stores (very inexpensive) or a camera store (more expensive), you can have some fun with your child.

Materials

A magnifying glass
A piece of paper
An inexpensive telescope (optional)

Directions: To demonstrate most dramatically how a telescope works, particularly if you have the inexpensive version, dismantle the telescope and take out the main objective lens (the one at the front of the telescope that gathers the light). Holding this lens with the fingertips of your left hand, which should be out-stretched, hold the eyepiece with the fingertips of your right hand

and bring it up to your eye. Look toward some distant object, like a road sign or a house, and aim the lenses at that object. Move your left hand in and out until the image is focused on the eyepiece in your right hand. Having your child do this will show him just how simple, yet powerful, the telescope is.

To your child:

Now you try the experiment. See that sign way down the street? Hold the big lens in your left hand like this [showing him], and the little lens in your right hand like this [showing him], and move the lenses in and out until you can see the sign clearly. See how big it looks? That's what telescopes do. They make faraway objects look bigger and closer.

Sound

4. WHAT IS SOUND?

To parents: Sound is the vibration of air, which creates waves of vibrating air, or sound waves. If there is no air, then there can be no sound. In spite of the great explosions heard in science-fiction movies, there is no sound in space or on the moon, because there is no air.

Materials

One 12" rubber band

Directions: Take a rubber band and hook it around anything stable, like a doorknob. Stretch the rubber band and have your child pull it from the side and let it go so that it makes a "twanging" sound. This sound is created by the vibration of the rubber band as it moves rapidly back and forth.

To your child:

Sound is air vibration. The sound of my voice, which you can hear now, is actually caused by my vocal cords vibrating, which makes the air vibrate, which makes your eardrums vibrate. You can hear the rubber band make a sound when you snap it because it is vibrating. Since there is no air on the moon, do you think there are sounds on the moon? That's right, there is no sound on the moon because there is no air. So when you hear spaceships blow up in science-fiction movies, that's not right, because there is no air in space either.

5.   WHY ARE SOME SOUNDS HIGH AND OTHERS LOW?

To parents: The highs and lows of sound are created by faster or slower air vibrations. Physicists call this "pitch." Sounds have different pitches. Fast vibrations create high sounds, so they have high pitch; slow vibrations create low sounds and so have low pitch.

Directions: Do the same experiment you did in number 4, but this time after your child snaps the rubber band have him remember what the pitch of the sound was like. Now stretch the rubber band out much farther and tighter. As your child will hear when he snaps it, the rubber band will vibrate faster and will have a higher pitch, so the sound will be higher. You have just changed the pitch of the sound. Your child can change the pitch up and down by stretching the rubber band tighter or looser.

To your child:

Sounds do not all "sound" the same. There are high sounds and low sounds. Physicists call these differences in sounds the "pitches" of the sounds. So there are high sounds, or sounds with high pitch, and low sounds, or sounds with low pitch. The vibrations that we already talked about cause sounds to be high or low. Fast vibrations cause high sounds. Slow vibrations cause low sounds. Let's do the same experiment with the rubber band, but this time we'll change the pitch by stretching it tighter or looser.

6.   CAN SOUND TRAVEL THROUGH THINGS OTHER THAN AIR?

To parents: As we saw in the first couple of experiments on sound, sound travels through air very well. But can it travel through other materials as well? Here are three experiments to help you and your child answer this question. The first one, which is the classic "telephone" experiment most of us did as children, will show your child whether sound can travel through string. In the second experiment, you'll determine whether sound can travel through water. And in the third, you'll see what else it can travel through.

Materials for #1

Can opener
Two tin cans
Scissors
String

Directions for #1: With the can opener, cut out one end of each of two tin cans, leaving the other ends intact. Punch a small hole in each of the other ends. Cut a roughly fifteen-foot-long piece of string. Attach one end of the piece of string to each of the two tin cans by knotting the string on the inside of the hole of each tin can. Now, each taking one of the tin cans, you and your child should move to a distance of about fifteen feet from each other. Have your child hold the tin can up to her ear. Now, shout fairly loudly into your tin can. Have her do the same to you. You should be able to hear each other's voices differently than you could if you were just standing fifteen feet apart and talking without using the tin-can "telephone." You have shown that sound can also travel through string. As an addition to the experiment, try cutting longer and longer pieces of string and see how far you can move apart before the string does not work very well anymore. How far apart did you get?

Materials for #2

Fish tank or large bowl
Two rocks

Directions for #2: Fill a fish tank or a large bowl with water. Have your child place his hand in the water and snap his fingers. Can he hear the sound? If he cannot snap his fingers, have him hold two rocks in the tank of water, one in each hand, and knock them together. The sound should be even better. If you have access to a swimming pool to do this experiment, the effect will be even more dramatic. Have your child go underwater in the shallow end and hold his breath for a few seconds (assuming he can swim) while you go under at the other end. Now, snap your fingers or strike two rocks together. He will be able to hear them quite clearly. In fact, the sound will even be better than if you were the same distance apart outside of the pool. So not only does sound travel in water, it travels better in water than in the air! This helps biologists explain how dolphins and whales can communicate so well over enormous distances in the ocean.

Materials for #3

Alarm clock (not a digital clock but a metal, vibrating clock)
Wooden stick
Metal stick

Directions for #3: Set up the alarm clock so that it goes off. Hold one end of the long wooden stick against the alarm clock and the other end up to your child's ear. She should be able to hear the sound through the wooden stick, since sound travels through wood. Next, hold a metal stick up to the alarm clock with the other end up to your child's ear. Not only should she be able to hear the sound, but she should be able to hear it better through the metal stick than she did through the wooden stick. Sound travels more easily through metal than through wood, because metal vibrates more than wood.

To your child:

Since sound is just air vibrating, do you think sound can be heard through other things that vibrate? You see, sound really is just vibration. When string vibrates, or water vibrates, or metal vibrates, or wood vibrates, they all make sounds. That's why you can hear me calling you from another room or outside. Sound goes through walls and windows. See how easy physics is?

Heat

7.   CAN YOU GAIN HEAT?

To parents: If you've ever had the experience of getting into a black car with a black interior on a hot summer day, then you already know that heat can be gained quite easily.

Materials

Two glasses of water
Black paper
White paper
Two rubber bands
Thermometer

Directions: Have your child take the two glasses of water and wrap one of them in black paper and the other in white paper, using the rubber bands to secure the paper to the glass. Next, have him set both of them in the shade for thirty minutes and then take the temperature of the water in each glass. (Meanwhile you can be doing other experiments.) The temperatures should be the same. Now have him put both glasses in the sun for thirty minutes. Take the temperatures again. The water in the glass wrapped in black paper should have a higher temperature than the water in the glass wrapped in white paper.

You can explain to your child that black absorbs the energy of light, while white reflects the energy of light. Light can create heat. The black paper absorbed the light energy and became warm; in this case, the heat was transferred from the paper to the water. So light energy in the form of heat cannot only be absorbed, thus causing a gain of heat, but it can also be transferred. As we'll see soon, the transferability of energy is extremely important.

To your child:

Heat can be caused by light energy, like that from the sun. Let's do an experiment to see whether something can get hotter by just being in the sun. [Do the experiment.] Black things soak up more heat than white things. This is because the color white "reflects" the heat, or makes it bounce off, while the color black "absorbs" the heat, or makes it get soaked up—sort of like a heat sponge.

8. CAN YOU LOSE HEAT?

To parents: If you've ever gone from your warm house to the out-of-doors on a cold winter day, you know how quickly you can lose heat. In fact, everything in the world is in the process of losing heat. As soon as you finish heating up food, it begins to cool down. A cup of hot coffee or cocoa cools down in a matter of minutes, if left standing. Even the sun is in the process of cooling down, but while it burns itself out over billions of years, it gives off lots of heat. Physicists call this the *second law of thermodynamics,* or *entropy.* This law says that everything in the universe is moving from a wide range of temperatures (very hot to very cold) to a single uniform temperature.

But what about things that get warmer, as in the experiment we just did? When you remove the heat source, after adding heat to interrupt the cooling process, whatever it was you were heating immediately begins to cool down again. Imagine how cold the earth would get if the sun were removed. (You can get some feel for this on a cloudy day, when the sun's rays are being blocked by clouds.)

Some things lose heat faster than others, depending on the surface area of the object or on how much of its surface is exposed to the air. The more surface area, the faster the heat loss. Let's see how this works.

Materials

Two glasses of water
Two ice cubes
Hammer

Directions: Fill two glasses with water from the kitchen tap, making sure that the water temperature is the same in both glasses (just leave the faucet in the same position for both glass fillings). Break one ice cube into many small pieces with the hammer and put the pieces into one of the glasses of water. Leave the other ice cube whole and place it in the second glass of water. Observe which cube—whole or broken—melts completely first. As you will see, the pieces of ice melt much faster than the whole ice cube—long after the pieces have melted in the first glass, the cube will still be there.

The reason for this is that all the little pieces of ice add up to much greater surface area than the one large piece of ice. This greater surface area allows more of the water to touch the ice, thus melting it. With the whole ice cube, the outer part of the cube must melt first before the water can get to the ice inside.

This experiment explains a lot of things. It explains, for instance, why it is so important for your child to wear gloves in cold weather. Her little fingers have much more surface area in proportion to their volume than, say, her arm does. Therefore, her fingers have relatively more surface area exposed to the cold. More relative surface area means a faster exchange of heat, so fingers get cold faster than arms, toes faster than legs, and ears and noses faster than heads.

You can introduce your child to the world of physical anthropology with this experiment by explaining that different groups of people around the world have different features and different skin colors, depending on the climate where they live. For example, Eskimos have flattened noses, ears, and faces, and small fingers and toes. They live in such cold climates that they evolved these special features to help them stay warm. In contrast, native Africans and Australian Aborigines tend to be tall and lanky, with long fingers and toes and well-defined noses and ears, because it is so hot where they live that they need to lose heat quickly.

(Perhaps you are wondering why natives of Africa and Australia tend to be dark skinned and natives of colder climates tend to be light skinned, not the other way around, since dark colors absorb heat and light colors reflect it. The reason is that darker skin colors evolved as a protection against the sun's harsh ultraviolet radiation. Darker skin is more protective than lighter skin, acting as a sort of permanent tan.)

To your child:

If things can gain heat, they can also lose heat. [Do the experiment.] The ice melted because the water was warmer than the ice. The ice got warmer but the water got cooler, because heat can be both gained and lost. But did you notice that the ice in the two glasses didn't melt at the same speed? Which one melted first—the whole ice cube, or the small chunks of ice? Why do you think the small chunks of ice melted first? The reason is that more of the surface area of the little pieces of ice is touching the water, so these pieces melt faster. With the big piece of ice, there is a lot more ice inside the cube that the water can't touch. Your fingers get cold faster than your arms because they are smaller; since there isn't as much inside to keep them warm, the air makes them cold faster. Do you know what Eskimos look like? They have small fingers and little noses and ears because it is very cold where they live and this helps them stay warm.

Energy

9. HOW DOES ENERGY CHANGE?

To parents: This is going to be a thought experiment, because you won't really see much happening. You and your child will have to imagine this experiment. Einstein did a lot of these imagination experiments; he had a great imagination, which helped make him a great scientist.

Materials

One wind-up toy

Directions: Have your child wind up the toy and then let it do its thing. When it has run out, you might try having the following sort of question-and-answer conversation to teach your child about this principle of energy. (It won't go exactly this way, of course, and your child may not be able to answer in exactly this manner, so you may need to direct his answers toward the next question.)

To your child:

PARENT: "What made the wind-up toy move?"

CHILD: "The spring inside." (If he doesn't already know this, you can take the toy apart and show him.)

PARENT: "What made the spring unwind?"

CHILD: "It got wound up."

PARENT: "How did it get wound up?"

CHILD: "I wound it up."

PARENT: "How did you wind it up?"

CHILD: "I wound it up with my fingers."

PARENT: "What made your fingers move?"

CHILD: "The muscles in my fingers and my arm."

PARENT: "Where did you get the energy to move the muscles in your fingers and arm?"

CHILD: "From breakfast this morning."

PARENT: "What did you eat for breakfast?"

CHILD: "I had a banana."

PARENT: "Where did the banana come from?"

CHILD: "From a banana tree."

PARENT: "What do all trees need in order to grow?"

CHILD: "Sunshine."

PARENT: "You see, the energy from the sun made the banana tree grow, which produced the banana fruit, which you ate to give your muscles energy to be able to wind up the toy so that the spring can make it work. So all energy comes from the sun and gets changed from one source to another, and another, and another."

Regardless of the exact conversation you have, the main point to be made is that energy is changeable, and that *all* of the energy we use ultimately comes from the sun. This is why we'd be in big trouble if the sun were to burn out now.

ASTRONOMY

Astronomy is the branch of science that deals with the motion of and relationships among the heavenly bodies, such as planets, stars, galaxies, and all the components that make up the universe. Most interesting to children are experiments that demonstrate the relationship of the earth to the moon, the sun, and the other planets, as well as how these interactions affect us on earth. We will do a number of experiments that show some of the basic principles of astronomy.

10.   WHAT CAUSES THE SEASONS?

To parents: At the beginning of this chapter, we saw how misleading such an apparently simple question can be. I explained that the seasons are caused by the tilt of the earth's axis in relation to its orbit, but I am uncertain whether anyone reading this can really visualize what is happening. Figure 3 will help, since it's two-dimensional. Better still would be a trip to a planetarium to see a working 3-D model, showing the sun casting light on the earth as it revolves in its orbit. But you can do a simple experiment in your living room to demonstrate the same thing.

This is 3-D science at its best. As one teacher using the STAR method says, "To convert from three dimensions to two and back to three again leads to special reasoning ability." Note that it doesn't *require* special reasoning ability, but rather *leads* to it. That is one of the goals of this book.

Materials

A light bulb (with no lamp shade)
A tennis ball or an orange
A felt-tip pen

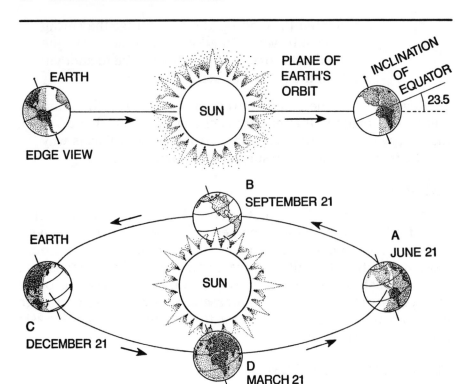

FIGURE 3

Directions: Turn off all the lights in the room except for one nondiffuse light (for example, a small table lamp with no shade). Take the tennis ball or orange, draw a circle around it to represent the equator, and two dots, one for the North Pole and one for the South Pole. Then draw a dot about one-third of the way up from the equator to represent a city in the United States (which sits about one-third of the way above the equator). Now tilt the ball slightly (to represent the 23.5-degree tilt of the earth).

Have your child hold the ball and walk in a circle around the lamp with you, keeping the dot facing the lamp but making sure the tilt stays the same—on one side of the orbit it will point toward the sun, on the opposite side away from the sun. As you make your way around the lamp, you will see that the light from the lamp on one side of the "orbit" is shining directly on top of the dot; on the other side it is shining on the dot from more of an angle. These two positions represent summer and winter.

At one end, the imaginary pole coming out of the North Pole will be pointing toward the sun (summer); at the other end, the imaginary pole coming out of the North Pole will be pointing away from the sun (winter). The day on which the sun is closest to being directly overhead at noon is the longest day of the year (the "summer solstice," June 21), and the day on which the sun is least directly overhead at noon is the shortest day of the year (the "winter solstice," December 21). The middle two positions represent autumn (September 21, the "autumnal equinox") and spring (March 21, the "vernal equinox").

As you do this experiment, keep your child continually aware of how the sun shines on the dot representing your city. Show her, too, that the North Pole points toward the sun during the summer and away from the sun during the winter.

11.   WHY DON'T WE EVER SEE THE BACK SIDE OF THE MOON?

To parents: In observing the moon with any regularity, it becomes obvious pretty quickly that we never see the back side of the moon. We always see the same side. Why? Astronomers call this phenomenon "the synchronous rotation of the moon." What this means is that the rotation of the moon (the "spinning" of the moon on its axis, like the spinning of a top) is in "synchronism" with the moon's revolution around the earth (its movement, or orbit, around the earth). In other words, it takes exactly 27.33 days for the moon to rotate once on its axis, and exactly 27.33 days for it to revolve once around the earth. If you lived on the moon, one "day" would equal 27.33 of our days. Figure 4 shows this quite clearly, and you can "prove" it to your child by doing the experiment that follows.

Materials

A beach ball
A tennis ball
A felt-tip pen

Directions: Have your child hold the beach ball, which will represent the earth, while you hold a tennis ball, which will represent the moon. Draw a big happy face on one side of the tennis ball to represent the "man in the moon." As the moon revolves around the earth (that is, as you walk in a circle around your

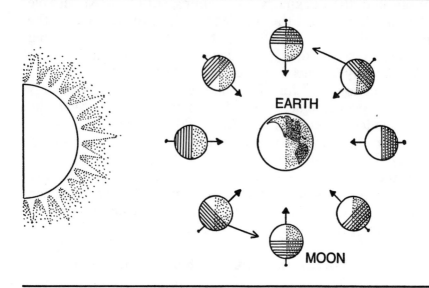

FIGURE 4. Synchronous rotation of the moon

child), it will rotate at a rate exactly matching that of its revolution. One side will thus always face the earth (that is, as you walk around your child, rotate the ball so that the "man in the moon" face is always pointing toward your child).

Make sure your child follows you around so that she always sees the face pointing toward her. (Her motion represents the rotation of the earth, but it *is not* in sync with the moon—rather, it is rotating once every twenty-four hours, making up a single day.) Explain to her as you proceed that the moon is always pointing toward the earth.

To your child:

Every time we look at the moon, we always see the same side of the moon. The "man in the moon" is always facing us. Have you ever seen the back side of the moon? No, and neither has anyone else, except in pictures brought back by spacecraft. We always see the same side of the moon because the moon is spinning at exactly the same rate as it goes around the earth. It takes a little over 27 days to spin once around, and a little over 27 days to go once around the earth. So if you lived on the moon, one day would be 27 of our days long! Let's try this experiment to see how that works.

12. How Do Rockets Get into Space?

To parents: The 3-D method of teaching science is so effective that a preschooler can learn one of Newton's laws of physics and at the same time understand how rockets get into space. Sound incredible? It is, but it's simple.

Newton's third law states: "To every action there is always opposed an equal reaction." These ten words are clear enough, but can your child *visualize* this concept? Figure 5 demonstrates it clearly, in an example that every child is likely to be familiar with—the launching of a rocket. When fuel burns, its atoms expand in all directions (as in an explosion). But since the side walls of the rocket are strong, the "explosion" can only go in one direction—toward the opening at the bottom. The "explosion" of the fuel is the action that pushes the rocket upward—the reaction.

Materials

A balloon

Directions: The simplest way to demonstrate Newton's third law is to have your child blow up a balloon and then release it. As the air rushes to escape from the small opening in the balloon— the *action*—the balloon *reacts* by shooting in the opposite direction. The reason it flies all over the room with no directional consistency is that it has no flying rudders to steer it. If rockets didn't have tail-fin stabilizers for guidance, they, too, would fly in all directions, as they did in the early days of rocketry experimentation.

To your child:

We're going to do an experiment that will show you one of the most important laws in all of physics. This law is the one that made it possible for people to make rockets go into space and to put a man on the moon. Isaac Newton is the person who discovered this law, which is that for every action there is a reaction—something just the opposite— that happens with equal power. For example, let's try blowing up this balloon and see what happens. [Do the experiment.] Do you know why the balloon flew all over the

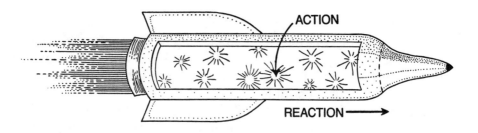

FIGURE 5

room? Because the air was rushing out of one end, pushing the balloon in the opposite direction.

13. WHAT CAUSES A SOLAR ECLIPSE?

To parents: A solar eclipse occurs when the moon passes between the sun and the earth in such a way that in areas of the earth within the shadow created by the moon, the sun is either partially or completely blocked, or "eclipsed." By pure coincidence, the relative "size" the moon appears to us at its distance from the earth (240,000 miles) is almost exactly the size that the sun appears to be at its distance from the earth (93 million miles). So when the moon passes in front of the sun, it blocks the sun's light almost completely. By all accounts, a total solar eclipse is supposed to be one of the most spectacular events of a lifetime. In the middle of the day it becomes quite dark. Flowers that normally close at night close during a solar eclipse, and stars can be seen. When the eclipse passes and the sun "returns," roosters crow as if it were morning.

For thousands of years, humans have known about solar eclipses. For most of that time, superstitious interpretations prevailed: a god was said to be destroying or eating the sun, or the eclipse was thought to be an omen of disasters soon to come. But as you can see in Figure 6, we now know that a solar eclipse is simply a shadow passing across the face of the earth. You can demonstrate this visually for your child.

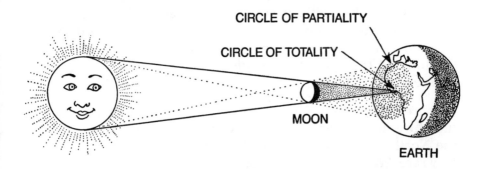

CIRCLE OF PARTIALITY

CIRCLE OF TOTALITY

MOON

EARTH

FIGURE 6

Materials

An unshaded lamp
A beach ball
A tennis ball

Directions: Place the lamp (representing the sun) in the center of a room. Have your child hold the beach ball, which will now represent the earth. The tennis ball, held by you, will represent the moon. Have your child stand about fifteen feet away from the lamp. Holding the tennis ball between your thumb and forefinger, pass it between the light and the beach ball so that the tennis ball casts a shadow on the beach ball. This shadow is like the shadow that is cast on the earth when the moon covers the sun during a solar eclipse. If you arrange the distance right, you can hold the tennis ball so that it exactly covers the light bulb to your child's eye. Do this and explain to him what is happening.

To your child:

One of the amazing coincidences in nature is that the moon and the sun appear to be almost exactly the same size in the sky. They aren't, of course. The moon is much smaller than the sun, but it is also much closer. The sun is huge, but is a long ways away. Every once in a great while the moon passes in front of the sun and causes a shadow to fall on the earth. If you were in that shadow, the sun would be blocked by the moon and it would get real dark, even in the middle of the day. It would be as if someone dimmed the lights for a while. Let's do an experiment to see how this happens.

Special note: Total solar eclipses are a fairly rare phenomenon in nature. Total solar eclipses in which the shadow passes across the North American continent (and is thus accessible to us) are *very* rare. What's more, it may be cloudy when eclipses take place, so we often miss them entirely. On July 11, 1991, a total solar eclipse will pass right across both the big island of Hawaii and Baja California, two areas that are very accessible areas to Americans and that are almost never cloudy during that month. Furthermore, astronomers have calculated that this will be the longest total eclipse until the year 2132, with more than seven minutes of total darkness. Anyone who has ever seen a total solar eclipse will tell you that it is *not* an event to miss.

14.   WHAT CAUSES THE PHASES OF THE MOON?

To parents: The phases of the moon are an astronomical phenomenon that is not difficult to understand *when you can see it.* Trying to describe this phenomenon in words is more difficult, but simply put, the phases of the moon are caused by the angles at which sunlight strikes the moon from our vantage point on the earth. One half of the moon is always lit; we see that half lit from these different angles. There are eight lunar phases: (1) new, (2) waxing crescent, (3) first quarter, (4) waxing gibbous, (5) full, (6) waning gibbous, (7) third quarter, and (8) waning crescent (see Figure 7). (*Waxing* means increasing in size; *waning* means decreasing in size.)

Materials

An unshaded lamp
A tennis ball

Directions: Put the light, representing the sun, in the center of the room. Make sure that *all* other lights are off in the room so that the full effect of this experiment can be seen. This time, your child will be the earth, and you will hold the tennis ball (repre-

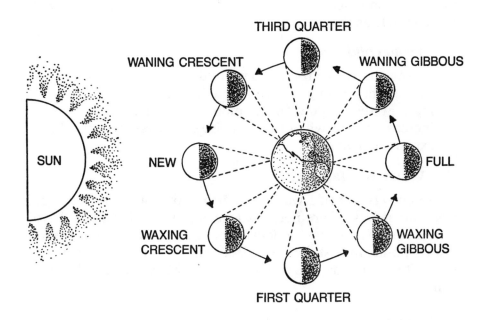

FIGURE 7

senting the moon) and walk in a circle around your child. When the moon is directly between the sun and the earth (your child), she won't be able to see it. But as you progress around her (in a counterclockwise motion, if looked at from above), she will be able to see a little "sliver," or crescent, of the moon (this is the waxing crescent).

As you continue to move, more and more of the moon will become lighted. When you are on the side of your child directly opposite the light, the entire moon will be lighted. This is a full moon. As you continue on, part of the moon will now start to disappear as less and less sunlight shines on it. When your child can see only half of the moon, it is in its third quarter. Finally, as you approach the position in which you began your circle around your child, a little sliver is all that can be seen. This is the waning crescent. When you return to your original position (where the moon can no longer be seen), this, once again, is the new moon. It's as simple as that!

To your child:

(As you walk around your child, keep asking her what she sees happening, and reinforce her verbally by explaining how the shadow on the moon is either decreasing or increasing. This will give her a visual understanding of the explanation above.)

15.   WHICH WAY IS NORTH?

To parents: When I was a Boy Scout, one of the first things I was taught was where north is located, in case I got lost. If you have a compass, it's easy to locate north, since the compass needle always points in that direction. But what if you don't have a compass? During the day, it's simple. At night, it's only a little bit more complicated.

Materials

None

Directions: If it is morning, you and your child should stand facing the sun. Since the sun always rises in the east, you are both facing east, so your child's left hand is toward the north. Have him lift his left arm straight out from his side, and tell him that his arm is pointing toward the north. Look to see what his left hand is pointing at, and note this as a landmark. Now have your child turn in the direction of that landmark so that he is facing north.

If it is late afternoon, have him face the sun as it sets in the west (but be sure he does not look directly at the sun). His right hand will be pointing north. Again, find a landmark toward which his right hand is pointing, and have him turn in that direction. Once again, he is facing north.

If you are doing this experiment in the middle of the day, finding north is a bit more difficult. Your child first has to get a track on the direction in which the sun is moving, so that he can see where it will set in the west. Putting a stick in the ground will cast a shadow. You can follow the movement of the shadow to see which way the sun is moving, which will be the opposite direction. When he has done so, follow the procedure for facing west, in the late-afternoon example just given.

At night, all you and your child have to do is locate the Big Dipper, which is one of the easiest constellations to find in the night sky. The diagram in Figure 8 will remind you of what it looks like. The Little Dipper constellation will also help you to locate the direction of north.

The Big Dipper has a "handle" and a "cup" that form the two parts of the constellation. Point this out to your child both in the diagram in Figure 8 and in the night sky. The two end stars in the cup generally point to Polaris, the North Star (which is also the end star in the "handle" of the Little Dipper). It's not an exact alignment, but Polaris is easily the brightest star in that general location. Its distance from the Big Dipper is about five times the distance between the two end, or pointer, stars in the Big Dipper.

Using these astronomical methods, your child will be able to tell where north is at any time of day or night. Astronomy is useful for locating not only points in space, but points on the earth as well.

CHEMISTRY

Chemistry is the science that examines the properties, composition, and structure of elements and compounds and how these can change, giving off or absorbing energy in the process. In other words, chemists try to figure out what things are made of and how some things can be changed into other things. They are not trying to change lead into gold, as alchemists did during the Middle Ages; instead, they are trying to understand how chemicals interact to affect both living and nonliving things.

We'll do five chemistry experiments to see some entertaining and enlightening results of chemical changes. If your child is interested in learning more about chemistry after you have done these experiments with her, a chemistry kit from a toy store would be a great place to start. These kits vary in complexity depending on the age range for which they are designed (generally, the levels start at age three and move up to high-school age). When I was boy my parents bought me a chemistry set, with which I amused myself for hours on end. With the number of

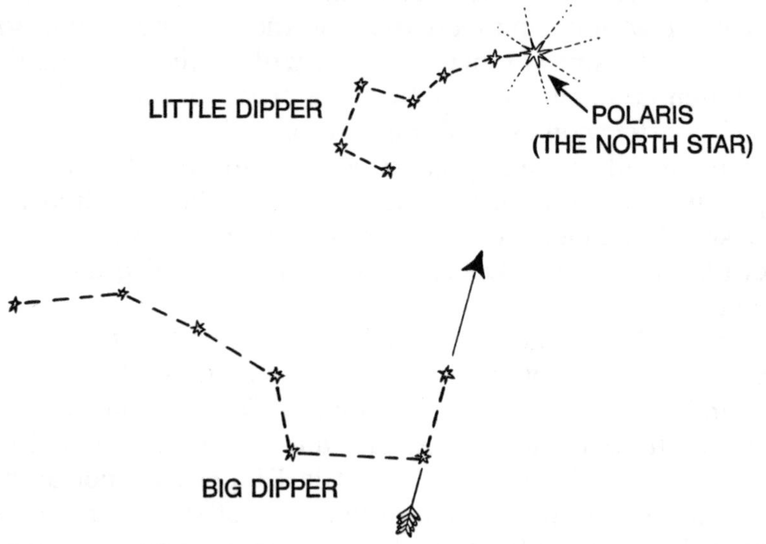

LITTLE DIPPER

POLARIS
(THE NORTH STAR)

BIG DIPPER

FIGURE 8

different types of chemicals, papers, and other tools that are included in such kits, there is an almost infinite variety of things that can be done. Instruction booklets explain the basic experiments to be conducted.

Even if the child just wants to tinker around and play with the parts of the kit, sort of trying things willy-nilly—which is mostly what I did with my kit—she will still learn manipulation skills and the handling of chemicals and scientific apparatus, and will gain a three-dimensional understanding of cause-and-effect relationships between various elements of the environment. For example, I learned a lot about chemistry by mixing different chemicals and pouring them on paper to see what sorts of reactions I could come up with that were not in the instruction booklet. Care should obviously be taken to avoid destroying valuable household goods and furniture, and supervision is recommended to avoid injury.

16. WHAT MAKES A FIRE BURN?

To parents: For many centuries chemists thought that when a candle burned, what was burning was a substance called "phlogiston" (from a Greek word meaning "to set on fire"). The German seventeenth-century physician and chemist Georg Stahl thought things that burned well were rich in phlogiston, and that when they burned they were consuming their supply of this substance; when the supply ran out, no more burning took place. The remaining ash of a piece of wood, for example, was out of phlogiston. Eventually, it was discovered that oxygen, not phlogiston, is what makes a flame burn. But so strong was the belief in phlogiston that Joseph Priestley, the eighteenth-century clergyman and chemist who discovered oxygen, called oxygen "dephlogisticated air."

Materials

A candle
A shallow metal pan
A tall glass

Directions: With a lighted candle, drip some wax into the bottom of the pan. Press the candle into the wax, and fill the pan with water. Now have your child take the tall glass and place it over the candle so that the rim of the glass is completely submerged in the water. Watch what happens to the flame and the water, and then ask your child what he has observed.

The first thing he will notice is that the flame goes out very quickly. This is because there is a limited supply of oxygen in the glass (and no more can get in because of the water), and the candle consumes it quickly. But he will also notice something else: the water rises up inside the glass (about one-fifth of the way up). Why? Point this out to your child if he hasn't noticed it, and ask him why he thinks it happened. He won't know.

The answer is quite fascinating, and it proves that it is oxygen alone that causes a flame to burn. Air consists of 78 percent nitrogen, 21 percent oxygen, and 1 percent other gases. The flame consumes most of the oxygen (since that is what makes it burn), leaving about one-fifth "space" in the glass to be filled. What is there to take the place of the oxygen? You guessed it—water! What happens to the oxygen? It is converted to carbon dioxide and absorbed by the water.

To your child:

Do you know what makes a fire burn? It's the oxygen in the air that gets burned by the flame of a fire. We can test this by doing an experiment. [Do the experiment described.] Oxygen makes up about one-fifth of the air. Did you see what happened to the water? That's right—the water rose up inside the glass. It looks as though the water moved about one-fifth of the way up in the glass, so that must mean that it was the oxygen that burned, and not anything else.

17. WHAT MAKES INVISIBLE INK VISIBLE?

To parents: Making invisible ink is one of the easiest chemistry experiments you can do. Boys especially enjoy it because they can write "secret" notes a la James Bond.

Materials

Fresh lemon
Paper cup
Stove or hot plate
Toothpick
Paper

Directions: Have your child squeeze the juice of a lemon into a paper cup. Then have him use the toothpick as a pen, dipping it into the lemon juice and then writing a message or drawing some sign or symbol on the piece of paper. Allow the juice to dry. Then hold the paper over the stove or the hot plate, being careful not to burn either yourself or the paper. The invisible "ink" will suddenly become visible.

Point out to your child that when lemon juice dries it cannot be seen easily unless it is held at a particular angle. Heating the dried lemon juice causes the acids in the juice to change into a brown color. This experiment shows that heat can be a causative agent in chemical change. This is why you always see Bunsen burners and gas stoves in chemistry labs.

To your child:

Let's make some invisible ink and write a secret message. [Do the experiment above.] As you can see, the ink is invisible before we heat it, but we can read it afterward. The reason is that heat changes chemicals. It makes them become something different. Sometimes chemicals even change color. In this experiment, we saw that lemon juice was changed from being an invisible color to a brown color.

18. How Do Crystals Grow?

To parents: Crystals are among the most fascinating shapes in nature and are one of the more interesting phenomena of chemistry. The shape of the atoms of the substance that makes a crystal actually shapes how the crystal looks.

Materials

A brick or some charcoal briquettes

Hammer

Cereal bowl

1/4 cup table salt

1/4 cup liquid bluing or bleach

1/4 cup water

1 tablespoon ammonia

Medicine dropper

Food coloring

Magnifying glass

Directions: Use the hammer to break the brick or the charcoal briquettes into small pieces. Have your child place several pieces in the cereal bowl. Mix the salt, liquid bluing (or bleach), water, and ammonia together in a separate bowl, and have your child pour the solution over the pieces of brick or charcoal. Fill the medicine dropper with food coloring, and have your child drop small amounts over the brick pile. Let the bowl sit for a while to let the crystals grow. The crystals will crumble easily, so try not to move the dish around. *Warning:* Mixing liquid bleach and ammonia in small quantities is safe; however, breathing in the mixture in large quantities can be dangerous.

Watch to note when the first crystals appear and how fast they have developed, and have your child describe what he sees in as much detail as possible. Crystals are formed when the water is drawn into the brick, leaving the solids behind. The ammonia, bluing, and salt form a complex crystal. Using a magnifying glass will help your child to observe the particular shape of the crystal. Different substances form different crystals—for example, instead of salt you could try borax, Epsom salts, copper sulfate, or sodium hyposulfite. With a magnifying glass your child can easily see the differences among the crystal shapes.

To your child:

Atoms are the smallest things in the universe. They are so small that you can't see them even with the most powerful of microscopes. But when a bunch of atoms get together, they sometimes make little structures called crystals. Crystals are like little buildings with straight sides and sharp angles. [Do the experiment.] Can you describe all the different shapes of crystals that you see? They look different because different atoms are of different shapes. So, in a way, we've just been looking at atoms through the magnifying glass!

19. How Does a Gas Expand?

To parents: As we saw in Experiment 17 with the invisible ink, chemists use heat as a catalyst (an agent of change) to change chemical structures. As molecules of a substance—whether that substance is a solid, a liquid, or a gas—are heated, they move faster and faster and expand the substance. In the following experiment you can show your child how this happens with a gas—air.

Materials

Balloon
Test tube
Candle
Tongs

Directions: Pull the end of a small balloon over the opening of an empty test tube. Have your child use the tongs to hold the test tube over a flame, which will cause the balloon to expand. Point out to your child that the test tube wasn't empty after all—it had a gas in it. That gas is called air. The heat expanded the air, causing it to rise into the balloon and make it expand. Then let the test tube cool and you'll see the balloon contract as the air cools.

To your child:

Remember the experiment we did earlier with the invisible ink, and how heat changed the ink? Heat is a very powerful thing. It makes lots of things change. [Do the experiment.] See how heat changed a gas? In this experiment, the heat made the atoms move around really fast and caused them to expand. That's what made the balloon get big. Heat is very important in chemistry.

20.   WHAT IS EVAPORATION?

To parents: Water molecules are constantly moving in all directions and at different speeds. The molecules of surface water in a lake, stream, or dish are moving so fast that they sometimes escape into the air as vapor—in other words, a liquid changes into a gas. Water becomes water vapor through the process of evaporation. If you've ever set up a fish tank and left it standing for a while, you've noticed that you have to put water in occasionally, especially if the tank doesn't have a top. Where did this water go? It went into the atmosphere. The rate of evaporation depends on several factors. Heat, of course, is one of these factors, but there are others, as we shall see in the next three experiments that will show us the various conditions under which evaporation occurs.

Materials for #1

Two pans
Cup
Water
Stove

Directions for #1: Have your child pour a cup of water into one of the pans, and set it to one side. Then have him put a cup of water in the second pan. Place this pan over a source of heat (your stove set on "medium" will do) for a half-hour. At the end of that time, you and your child can measure the amount of water left in both pans. The one that was heated evaporated faster because, as we saw in previous experiments, heat causes chemicals to change and causes molecules to move faster, both of which happen in evaporation. Boiling water makes the evaporation happen even faster.

Materials for #2

Cup
Water
Empty olive jar
Bowl
Cake pan

Directions for #2: Have your child pour a cup of water into each of three different-sized containers—an olive jar, a bowl, and a cake pan. Let these stand for one day. The next day, have your child measure the amount of water left in each container. (Just pour them back into the original cup and mark the difference.) You and your child will notice that the amount of surface exposed to the air affects the rate of evaporation. The greater the surface area, the faster the evaporation.

Materials for #3

Cup
Water
Two pans
Electric fan

Directions for #3: Have your child pour a cup of water into each pan. Place an electric fan in front of one of the pans, and have your child put the other pan on the far side of the room, away from the breeze. Make sure that the two pans have equal surface areas and are of equal temperatures. (You can do this by just looking and estimating.) Turn the fan on for a couple of hours, then have your child measure the amount of liquid left in the two containers by pouring them back into the original cup and noting the difference. The water in the container with the fan will have evaporated faster, because the movement of air near the surface of a body of water increases evaporation.

To your child:

When water escapes from its source into the air, this is called evaporation. The water that goes into the air eventually comes down again as rain, after a lot of it has collected to form clouds. [Do the three experiments above.] As we saw, water will evaporate, or escape into the air, at different speeds. When the water gets hot it escapes faster. This is because heat, as we saw in the last experiment, makes atoms and molecules move faster. Also, when a lot of water is exposed to the air, it will escape faster because more is coming into contact with the air—just as the little pieces of ice melted faster than the whole cube in the earlier experiment we did, because the pieces had more surface area touching the water. Wind also makes water escape faster, because it pushes the little molecules on the surface into the air faster.

BIOLOGY

Biology is the study of life. Evolution is the study of how life changes and adapts to a changing environment. We will do some fun experiments to see how the world of life is constructed so that your child can better understand the rich world of living organisms that surrounds us and of which we are a part.

21. HOW DO ANIMALS EVOLVE?

To parents: Animals have very basic functions in living. They must eat, sleep, and reproduce. In turn, they must avoid being eaten themselves! Many animals protect themselves by being camouflaged so that they look like their environment. When the environment changes, the camouflage of the next generation of animals also changes. That is, those animals that no longer look like the newly changed environment are more likely to get eaten; those that look like the new environment don't get eaten, so they can reproduce more little animals that look like them. This, in a nutshell, is how evolution works. The process just described is called *adaptation*. A species adapts to its environment by changing. Change is what evolution is all about.

This experiment will show this graphically to your child, as you and she invent an animal that is adapted to a specific environment.

Materials

Potatoes
String beans
Carrots
Cotton
Glue
Toothpicks
Colored poster paints
Paintbrushes of different sizes

Directions: Take all the materials to a local park or to some other area that is grassy or leafy. Have your child "invent" an animal out of the materials by creating an animal that is camouflaged so that it is hard to see. She will probably first put an animal together from the vegetable parts, maybe using the potato as the body, carrot sticks as the legs, cotton for hair, and so on. But as it is, this animal is pretty easy to spot sitting in some leaves. So the next step is to have your child paint the animal so that it blends in with the environment—in other words, so that it is camouflaged.

To make a fun game out of this experiment, you might try having your child put the animal in some leaves, grass, or twigs while you keep your eyes closed. Count to ten, as in a game of hide-and-seek, and then try to find the animal. If she has painted it well, it will not be easy to spot. Have her make lots of different animals until the materials run out.

To your child:

Animals have evolved in order to be good at survival. Those that weren't good at it got eaten and didn't live long enough to have babies. Those that were good at survival did live long enough to have babies, and these grew up better adapted to their environment. One of the important ways to adapt to your environment is to be camouflaged so that other animals don't see you. Let's do an experiment where we'll make an animal so that he is well camouflaged and hard to see.

22. How Do Plants Evolve?

To parents: One of the ways that animals can adapt to their changing environments is by moving. If the environment is too hot, too cold, or too dry or there isn't enough food or water, an animal can just move to a location where the environment is better and where food and water are available. Since, unlike animals, plants cannot move, they must evolve and adapt to their environments in a different way from that used by animals. Plants evolve special types of leaves, stems, or branches that are particularly suited to the local climate. The biological study of plants is called botany.

This time, you and your child will invent plants that are adapted to a specific environment. This experiment will help your child to understand evolution in a way different from that learned in the previous experiment.

Materials

Liquid plastic film (for example, Fantasy Film, Fun Film, Form-a-Film, or cellophane)

Synthetic plant materials from a hobby shop or florist who sells synthetic plants

Roll of floral tape

Scissors

Thin aluminum wire

Small piece of Styrofoam

Clay

Egg-carton base

Directions: Go to a park or to some local hills or woods and make some observations about the different types of trees, ferns, bushes, and other plants there are. Then find an open area or picnic table where you can construct your own plants. Using the materials listed above, you and your child can build different plants with different adaptations to local conditions. Use the Styrofoam, clay, or egg carton as a base for holding the home-made plant trunks upright.

For example:

Build a plant that can live on the surface of a pond. This would be shaped so that it would float.

Build a plant that an animal would have a hard time eating. This could be made with many small, sharp wires sticking out from the stem of the plant like thorns.

Build a plant to catch insects. You might try building a plant with leaves that curl upward and have little spines on the top of each edge, so that if you closed the curled leaf the spines would overlap, like interlocked fingers. This is how the Venus flytrap plant works.

Build a flower that will attract bees and insects. This one might have leaves that are very colorful and have been painted to look a little like a bee or another insect in order to attract a real bee or insect.

Build a tree that can withstand strong winds. This might have a really thick trunk with many sturdy branches and small leaves so that not too much surface area is presented to the wind.

This is a good exercise in imagination. Creating models of plants that resemble real ones will teach your child to be an excellent observer of nature. By becoming better observers, we can learn to see life in a different light.

To your child:

Plants evolve just like animals. Those that are best able to survive leave behind the most offspring. But since plants can't move like animals, they have to make special kinds of changes in order to survive. They grow special types of leaves, stems, or branches that adapt to the local environment. Let's do an experiment where we'll make different types of plants that are adapted for different types of environments.

23. HOW MANY WAYS ARE THERE TO ADAPT?

To parents: Take your child to the local zoo. At the zoo, play a guessing game to help your child understand the many different ways there are for animals to evolve and adapt to their environments.

Materials

None

Directions: Just walk around the zoo with your child (which is a fun experience even if you're not doing an experiment), and play the following guessing game with him: for every animal you come up to, have your child guess—without reading the sign that explains everything about that animal—why the animal looks like it does. Does it have long hair or short hair? Sharp teeth or flat teeth? How many legs does it have? What color is it? In what way is it camouflaged? Does it fly or walk or swim? Does it live in the desert or the mountains? Does it live in a cold climate or a hot climate? Does it have claws? Does it eat plants or animals?

Then read the sign that explains where the animal is from, what it eats, and in what ways it is adapted to its environment. These adaptations are the end products of that animal's evolution.

To your child:

In this experiment we'll see how animals have evolved by actually looking at animals in the zoo from all over the world. When we see an animal let's look at how long his hair is, whether he has sharp teeth or flat teeth, what color he is, what type of camouflage he has and so on. Then we'll guess what type of climate he lives in and where he came from. We'll try to guess if he is from a warm climate or cold climate, what type of food he eats, and if he is a predator or a prey animal.

24. How Do Plants Grow?

To parents: Most of the time we don't see plants (or animals, for that matter) grow, because the growing process is so slow and gradual. Nature does not make leaps. Change tends to be painstakingly slow for those observers called biologists. To note and observe the growth of a plant, for instance, you can set up special experiments so that your child can make a daily recording of a plant's growth.

Materials for #1

Dry lima beans
Water
Empty egg cartons with tops cut off
Planting soil

Directions for #1: In this experiment you will plant a lima bean every day in one of the holes in the egg carton. At the end of 12 days you'll have 12 plants growing, each at a different stage of development.

Each day soak the lima bean in water overnight. Put a little soil in each egg carton hole, placing the lima bean about one-fourth to one-half inch below the surface of the soil. Have your child water each seed daily. Make a chart on a piece of paper to record her observations of what has happened each day. Note what happens to the seed, how many leaves develop, how tall the plant becomes, and so on.

Materials for #2

Paper
Avocado
Toothpicks
Glass of water

Directions for #2: Cut the avocado open, remove the seed and wash it in water. Take four toothpicks and push them into the seed around its center. Then put the avocado seed in a glass of water so that the toothpicks hold it on the rim of the glass. Put in enough water that about one-half to three-fourths of the seed is immersed in water. As in the previous experiment, make a chart on which your child can note her observations each day.

From these experiments your child will be able to observe the slow and steady development of an organism from a seed to a full-fledged plant—truly the miracle of life!

To your child:

All plants and animals grow, just like you are growing and getting bigger all the time. But growth is such a slow process that we usually can't see it happening. In this experiment we'll plant some lima bean seeds, one each day, and then we'll see the steady progress of growth. In the end we'll have an egg carton filled with baby plants at all different stages of growth.

EARTH SCIENCE

The earth sciences cover a number of subjects relating to the earth and its environments, including geology, oceanography, geography, mineralogy, meteorology (weather), and paleontology (fossils). We'll do five experiments to see what sorts of things earth scientists study.

25. WHAT IS A FOSSIL?

To parents: A fossil is a trace of an organism left in the ground. That trace may be a footprint, an indentation, or the actual organic remains of the plant or animal. But most likely, a fossil will be none of these. Most fossils are "mineralized." That is, the original organic bone or shell, for instance, has disintegrated and been replaced by minerals from the ground. The replacement occurs slowly, over a long period of time, so that while the original material is gone, an exact mold of the organism still exists. No dinosaur bones are original "bone." They are all mineralized fossils—replaced and hardened over millions of years of lying in the ground. To see how this process works, you and your child can create your own fossil.

Materials

Clay
Knife
Soap
Seashell
Pencil
Plaster of Paris (or heated wax)

Directions

1. Form the lump of clay into a rectangle about two inches thick, four inches wide, and eight inches long.
2. With the knife, slice the clay rectangle in half lengthwise (leaving a "top" and "bottom" of the rectangle), then brush both sides with soapy water so they will be easier to pull apart after they have been pushed back together.
3. Take a seashell and press it into half of the clay rectangle.
4. Place the second half of the clay rectangle on top of the first and press down.
5. Pull the two halves apart and take out the shell. You should have two halves of a whole seashell cast.
6. Take the pencil and press it into the clay so that it makes a groove from the edge of the clay to the seashell cast.
7. After brushing the two halves with soapy water once again, put the two halves together, without the shell or pencil.
8. Mix up a batch of plaster of Paris (or heat some wax), to a thickness that can be poured. It should not be too watery, since it has to become hardened. Pour the mixture into the pencil hole so that the seashell cast is filled to become a mold. Tap it gently to remove any air bubbles.
9. After about ten to fifteen minutes, the plaster of Paris should be hardened. Pull the two halves of clay apart, and you will have a plaster-of-Paris mold of a seashell.

To find real fossils, call the natural history museum closest to where you live (see Appendix 4), and ask where in your area you could take your child fossil hunting. Fossil hunting is free, easy, and fun for a child. You never know what the next shovelful of dirt might reveal.

To your child:

This is, in a way, what a fossil is like. The original material is replaced by another, sturdier material, though in nature it takes hundreds of thousands, or even millions, of years for the process to occur. Understanding how fossils are made is critical to earth scientists and paleontologists because this is how they understand the evolution of life, the movement of the earth's continents, and the age of the earth. In fact, the various "epochs" of earth time (geological time) that geologists and paleontologists use are based on the types of fossils found in specific layers of rock. For example, it was from fossils that geologists learned one of the most amazing facts about nature ever discovered. The tallest mountain in the world, Mount Everest, has fossils of marine life at the top. This means that Mount Everest was once under water. Since there isn't enough water on the planet to reach that high, Mount Everest must have been pushed upward by the earth's forces.

26.   HOW OLD IS THE EARTH?

To parents: This is one of the most fundamental questions of all the earth sciences. It has been pondered for hundreds of years. In 1650, for instance, Bishop James Ussher of Ireland calculated that the creation of the heavens and the earth occurred in the year 4004 B.C., on October 23, a Friday, at 9:00 A.M. We've come a long way in our calculations of the age of the earth since Bishop Ussher's time, and the earth had already been around for a long time before 4004 B.C. Through the science of radioactive dating we now know that the earth was created approximately 4.6 billion years ago. It's nearly impossible for us to conceive of how long ago this was. After all, we're accustomed to thinking in terms of weeks, months, years, and decades. Anything older than a century is history. Anything older than a millennium (1,000 years) is practically ancient history. Ten thousand years ago, people were just beginning to farm. A million years ago? A billion years ago?? It's unimaginable . . . almost.

Materials

A 37-foot roll of adding-machine paper

Ruler or yardstick

Pen

Directions: Roll out the strip of adding-machine tape. With the ruler (or a yardstick, which will make this easier) mark off 12 lines, three feet apart, leaving an extra foot at the end. Have your child help by numbering each line. Write the name of the month above the line. This will represent the "Cosmic Calendar," invented by Carl Sagan, in which each "day" of the "month" represents approximately 50 million years! With your child helping out, write down the following significant dates on the Cosmic Calendar at where they would fit, approximately, for each month (e.g., September 14 would be marked about halfway between the September and October lines):

> *January 1:* The Big Bang—the beginning of the universe
> *May 1:* The creation of the Milky Way Galaxy (our galaxy)
> *September 9:* The creation of our solar system
> *September 14:* The origin of the earth
> *September 25:* The creation of life on earth
> *October 2:* Oldest dated rocks on earth
> *October 9:* Oldest bacteria fossils
> *November 12:* Oldest plant fossils
> *December 16:* First worm fossils
> *December 18:* Trilobites
> *December 19:* First fish
> *December 21:* First insects
> *December 22:* Rise of the amphibians (frogs, salamanders)
> *December 24:* Evolution of the dinosaurs
> *December 30:* Earliest ape-men

With the ruler, mark twelve inches on the final foot of the tape to represent human history and cultural evolution.

> *December 31:*
> *11:00 P.M.:* Use of stone tools by ancient man
> *11:59:20 P.M.:* Beginning of farming; invention of the plow
> *11:59:51 P.M.:* Invention of the alphabet
> *11:59:52 P.M.:* Flourishing of Egyptian culture
> *11:59:53 P.M.:* Trojan War; invention of the compass
> *11:59:54 P.M.:* Iron Age
> *11:59:55 P.M.:* Ancient Greeks—Aristotle, Plato, Socrates
> *11:59:56 P.M.:* Birth of Christ

11:59:57 P.M.: Fall of Rome

11:59:58 P.M.: Crusades

11:59:59 P.M.: Renaissance; birth of modern science

January 1, first second of the new year: Space exploration

This exercise should leave a strong impression on both you and your child. It is truly incredible just how old the earth is, and how new and young what we consider to be history really is. Think about it. The earth isn't even created until three-quarters of the way through the Cosmic Calendar; there are hardly six weeks to go before the first plants evolve. Trilobites don't come on the scene until 352 days out of the 365 have elapsed. The most primitive of ape-men doesn't appear until the second to the last day. And it's December 31, at 11:00 P.M., before humans are even using stone tools!

The vastness of time is a difficult concept for any of us to grasp, especially children. That's why a visual demonstration like this can be so effective. When I was a student of evolutionary biology, the professor had us run up eight flights of stairs. Along the railing was painted a time line, similar to the one you just constructed with your child. The professor told us to stop climbing stairs when we got to the Stone Age. We all figured we'd get to stop and rest by the fifth or sixth floor. Well, the Stone Age wasn't until the very top of the eighth floor, and we were exhausted! Time is indeed vast.

27. WHERE DOES RAIN COME FROM?

To parents: This may seem like it's going to be a difficult scientific question to answer. It isn't. Predicting when it's going to rain, on the other hand, *is* extremely difficult, as you may have noticed in watching the nightly weather-report predictions of television weathermen. But understanding where rain comes from is quite simple. The rain comes from the air, since air has water in it. When we say it's a humid day, we mean that the water content of the air is high; when it's a dry day, the water content is low.

Materials

One glass

Ice water

Directions: Fill a glass with ice water and let it sit for a few minutes. What happens? Before long, water droplets begin to form on the *outside* of the glass. Then they run down the sides and form a pool of water under the glass, marking up the coffee table!

To your child:

Where does the water on the outside of the glass come from? Maybe it comes from water in the glass. We can test this easily enough by marking the water level on the glass. But you can see that the water can't be leaking from the glass, because the water level in the glass stays the same. The water comes from the air. This is where rain comes from. Raindrops are formed in clouds where lots of tiny water droplets collide to form raindrops, or from falling snow that melts when it hits warmer air. When it gets cold, and there is more water in a cloud than the cloud can hold, it "leaks," or rains, the extra water out. You can see that air has water in it because this glass is all wet.

28.   WHAT IS A MAGNET?

To parents: You probably already know that the earth itself is a giant magnet, with a North Pole and a South Pole corresponding to the two opposite ends of the magnet. (Actually, the two magnetic poles of the earth have changed ends many, many times over the last several million years. They even wander about, never staying in the exact location for very long. Therefore, the geographic North Pole is not exactly the magnetic North Pole.) Surrounding every magnet is a magnetic field in which invisible lines of force operate. Everything that is influenced by magnetism and that is within this field will be affected. You can show this invisible force to your child by means of a very simple experiment.

Materials

One sheet of glass
Several pieces of paper
Two bar magnets
One horseshoe magnet
Iron filings

Directions: Place the sheet of glass or a piece of paper over the bar magnet and have your child sprinkle iron filings over it. The filings will arrange themselves in a pattern. On another piece of paper you could have your child draw a simple picture of what the pattern looks like. You can do the same thing using two bar magnets with the unlike poles together. This will produce a different pattern that you could have your child draw. The horseshoe magnet will produce still another type of pattern.

To your child:

This is an experiment on magnetism. Certain types of metals are magnetic—that is, they attract other types of metal to them. These magnets actually have a force field around them. You can see this force field when we do this experiment. See, different shape magnets give off different shapes of force fields. It's amazing that a piece of metal can have an invisible force surrounding it—but we've just proven it!

29. How Far Away Is a Thunderstorm?

The speed of sound and the speed of light are very different. Sound travels at a speed of about 700 miles per hour, or one-fifth of a mile per second, while light travels about 186,000 miles per second. So sound only goes about one-fifth of a mile in the same time it takes light to travel 186,000 miles, or seven times around the earth! You and your child can see and hear this difference the next time there is a good thunderstorm.

Materials

One thunderstorm, with a lot of lightning!

Directions: The instant you see the lightning (and for all intents and purposes, it will be instantaneous—no matter how far away the storm is, light is so fast that it reaches you at virtually the same time the lightning happens), have your child start counting off the seconds by saying "one thousand and one, one thousand and two, one thousand and three," and so on until the sound of the thunder is heard. A count of five means that the lightning was about one mile away. If you continue with the counting routine, you and your child will be able to tell whether the storm is moving toward you or away from you. You can also see this effect of the differential speeds of sound and light at a baseball game if you are sitting far enough away from home plate. You can see the batter swing before you hear the bat hit the ball.

The principle is the same—light travels so much faster than sound that events don't seem to happen at the same time.

To your child:

Let's see if we can tell how far away the lightning is in the storm. As soon as you see the lightning, begin counting "one thousand and one, one thousand and two, one thousand and three" until you hear the sound of the thunder. The lightning is causing the thunder, and the lightning and thunder are actually happening at virtually the same time, but light travels so much faster than sound that we see the lightning much sooner than we hear the thunder. Sound travels about one-fifth of a mile in a second, but light would travel seven times around the earth, or 186,000 miles in a second! Wow!! Light is much faster than sound.

PSYCHOLOGY

Psychology is the scientific study of human behavior. It's the science that tries to understand people and the many things that influence the way they act and think. We'll do six experiments that reveal some interesting things about ourselves.

30.   How Do Your Body and Mind Tell Temperature?

To parents: One of the first things any beginning psychology student learns is how the senses (sight, hearing, touch, taste, and smell) work and how they can be deceived. It seems as though our senses work just fine, but if you alter the conditions just a little, it's easy to fool the senses. Fooling the senses also tells us how the senses work.

Materials

Three glasses of water

Directions: In this experiment, fill three glasses with water as follows: fill the first glass with hot (but not scalding) water, the second glass with tepid (lukewarm) water, and the third glass with cold water. Have your child place a finger of his left hand in the first glass and a finger of his right hand in the third glass, keeping them there for thirty seconds. Now have him place the same two fingers in the second glass, and ask him how the water feels. What should happen is that the water in the second glass feels hot to the right finger and cold to the left finger. Why? Because the sense of temperature can be misled if we set up preconditions that are different for each finger. The finger that was in the hot water was conditioned to sense "hot," so when it was then put into tepid water, that water seemed "cold" by comparison. The finger that was in the cold water was conditioned to sense "cold," so when it was put in the lukewarm water, that water seemed "hot" by comparison. So the perception of temperature is a *psychological* phenomenon, not a physical one, and our senses are best at determining differences in the environment, not absolute standards.

To your child:

You can tell when water is hot or cold, can't you? Our bodies sense temperature because we have little temperature sensors in our skin. [Do the first part of the experiment, with one finger placed in hot water and one in cold.] You can tell which one is hot and which one is cold, right? [Now do the second part of the experiment.] Is this a glass of hot water or cold water?

The reason it feels hot to one finger and cold to another finger is that feeling temperature is not just done in the finger. It's also done up here [pointing to your child's head]. Our minds are wonderful machines, and they are very complicated. You see, your mind is confused right now about whether that glass of water [pointing to the glass in the middle] is hot or cold. Do you think that the water is both hot and cold? Of course not. Sometimes things may not be like what you *think* they are like. The temperature you feel may be caused by the temperature of your body. [Now have him dip two other fingers in the tepid water. The water will feel the same temperature to both fingers.] See, when both fingers are the same temperature, then the water feels the same.

31.   How Do We Taste Food?

To parents: If you've ever had a cold, then you know that taste is more than just a function of the tongue and the taste buds. Food tastes different when we are sick, and it has nothing to do with the cold affecting the sensory apparatus of taste. When we have a cold we usually can't smell things very well, if at all, and *this* is what makes food taste different.

Materials

Blindfold (optional)
Apple
Pear
Potato
Onion

Directions: Blindfold your child (or have her close her eyes) and have her hold her nose so she can't smell anything. Cut up small pieces of apple, pear, potato, and onion. Give her a piece of each to taste, one at a time, and each time have her guess which one she has just tasted. She will find it very difficult to tell the difference between the apple, pear, potato, and onion by texture and taste alone.

Without sight and smell, taste is a very indiscriminate sense. This experiment proves that without sight and smell, and world would taste very different. This experiment also proves that our senses do not act alone, but in conjunction with the other senses. Our senses are an integrated system for perceiving the world around us. The next time you catch a cold, remember this experiment!

To your child:

Do you think you could tell the difference between an apple, a pear, a potato, and an onion? [Of course, she should say. Now do the experiment.] You can't taste things so well when you can't see or smell them, can you? Remember when you were sick and things didn't taste very good? This is the same thing. This experiment proves that all of our senses [have her name them or point to them— eyes, ears, nose, tongue, and skin] work together.

32.   How Do We Tell Time?

To parents: This seems like a simple enough question. To tell the time, you just look at your watch. But if you didn't have a clock or a watch to look at, could you tell how much time has elapsed? Also, does time move at the same speed? Doesn't it seem to move faster when you are busy and slower when you are bored? Maybe time isn't just something recorded by a clock. In fact, the perception of time is a function of the human mind. It's our brain that tells time, not the clock. In this experiment you can test your and your child's abilities to tell time, and at the same time you can demonstrate that without a clock it's easy to distort time perception.

Materials

A watch or clock with a second hand

Directions: First, have your child hold the watch and tell you when the second hand reaches the twelve. Without counting seconds, when you think 30 seconds have elapsed declare your guess, and have your child tell you how you did. Now reverse the roles. You hold the watch and have your child guess when 30 seconds have elapsed. (Estimating one minute is better, but attention span can be a problem with this experiment.) To insure that your child is not counting, have the radio or television on, which usually interferes with thinking. This shows that it is difficult to tell time without a clock, but that we have *some* idea of the length of a certain period of time.

Now let's try something especially fun to prove whether being bored or interested makes time pass slower or faster. In this experiment, have your child estimate when he thinks one minute has elapsed. In the first part of the experiment you will read to him out of a dictionary—a reasonably boring pastime, by almost anyone's standards—and have him guess when he thinks one minute has elapsed. In the second part of the experiment, read to him out of a book he really enjoys and in which he is truly interested. Then have him guess when one minute has elapsed. (Again, if you could do it for several minutes it would be better.)

The results are likely to be quite different. Being bored makes time seem to pass much more slowly. When you drone on from the dictionary, your child is likely to guess that the minute is up long before it really is. (This is like being in a boring classroom lecture or business meeting, where you think it must be at least half over—and then you check the clock and find that only a few minutes have elapsed!) Being interested in something makes the time seem to pass much faster. When you are reading from something your child likes, he is likely to guess that the minute is up *after* it really is. (This is like being on a fun vacation, and you want it to last a long time—but the days on the calendar seem to fly by amazingly quickly.)

One of the things that make psychology interesting is that things happen that often surprise us. You wouldn't think that something as simple as time could be distorted by the human brain. As we shall see in the next experiment, time isn't the only thing that is fooled by the mind.

To your child:

Remember how much fun it was when you learned to tell time? We usually tell time by looking at a clock or a watch. But let's try a fun experiment where we will guess how much time has gone by without looking at a clock. [Do the first part of the experiment, estimating a 30-second period.] Now let's try another experiment, where you'll guess when one minute has gone by. [Do the second part of the experiment.] Look how different your two guesses were! It's hard to tell the time without a clock, isn't it? But our brains can really fool us. If we are bored the time seems to go slowly and if we are having fun the time seems to go fast. So time is not only what's on the clock, it's also what's up here [pointing to your child's head].

33. Is Seeing Believing?

To parents: As we saw in the last chapter, observation is the supreme court of appeal in science. "Show me" are two words that scientists live by. We trust our senses to tell us the truth about our environment. Yet, as psychologists tell us, and as we have seen in these first three experiments, things are not always as they appear. Seeing is not always believing.

Materials

The optical illusions in Figure 9

Directions: Show your child the optical illusions in Figure 9. Ask her the questions or follow the directions beneath each one, and see what sort of response she gives. Like everyone else, she should be deceived by these illusions.

More than just showing us how the mind can be tricked and that under certain conditions seeing is *not* believing, these optical illusions teach us something about how the visual system works. For example, in number one in Figure 9, you and your child should both have perceived the left line to be shorter than the

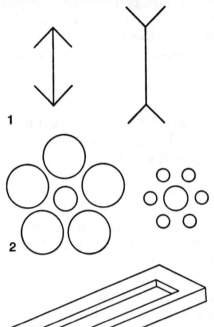

1. **Lines**: Which line is shorter, the line on the left within the arrows, or the line on the right between the arrows?

2. **Circles**: Which of the inside circles is larger, the inside circle on the left, or the inside circle on the right?

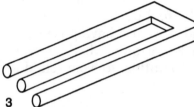

3. **Magical prongs**: How many prongs are there on the outside of this object? How many prongs are there when you look at it from the inside?

4. **Hidden figure**: Can you find the hidden figure among the black and white blotches?

FIGURE 9

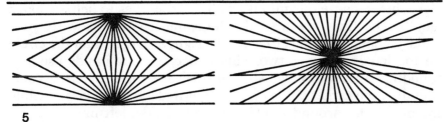

5

5. Curved lines: What do the horizontal lines appear to do on the left side of the figure? What do they appear to do on the right? What happens when you lay a ruler down to see if the lines curve?

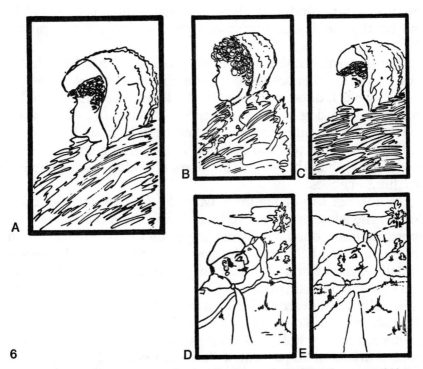

6

6. Old woman/Young woman: Look at the woman in B. What do you see? Now immediately look at the woman in A. What do you see? Look at the woman in C. Now look again at the woman in A. *Now* what do you see? Can you find the hidden figures in E? There are two. Now look at D, then back to E. *Now* can you find the hidden figures?

(See the text for explanations of all these illusions.)

FIGURE 9 (cont.)

right line, because our minds use the arrow cues to help us judge length. The lines are actually the same length. Likewise, your child probably saw the circle on the right as larger than the circle on the left in number two. This is because our minds use surrounding objects to judge size. In this case, the little circles surrounding the target circle on the right make it seem larger, while the big circles around the target circle on the left make it seem smaller. In fact, they are the same size. Use a ruler to actually measure the sizes, showing your child (who won't believe you) that they are actually the same size.

In number three, we are confused because on the outside of the object our minds are given cues for a three-pronged object, and on the inside our minds are given cues for a two-pronged object.

Try showing number four to your child and ask her what she sees. She will either see the dog immediately, or she will see just a bunch of black dots and blobs. If she doesn't see the dog, tell her that there is a dog in the picture. She should then see it immediately. Once the mind is given a concept to look for, it can find it. If it doesn't know what to look for, it goes into a sort of "search mode," looking at the picture and then checking memory to see if anything matches.

In number five of Figure 9, what do the two horizontal lines do? On the left they appear to bend inward, and on the right they appear to bulge outward. By placing a ruler or other straight edge across the length of the line, you will see that both lines are actually straight and that they are parallel. Have your child do this now. It's quite surprising.

Finally, in number six have your child first examine picture A. Does she see an old woman or a young woman? In experiments conducted by psychologists, 60 percent of subjects see the young woman first, and 40 percent see the old woman. Let's try another experiment. Picture B is a strong image of a young woman. Picture C is a strong image of an old woman. Have your child look first at picture B and then back at picture A, and ask her what she sees in picture A. She should see the young woman, because looking at picture B has set her mind up to look for the young woman (in the same way as in the dog picture, above). Now have her look at picture C and then back at picture A, and ask her what she sees in picture A. Now she should see the old woman, because looking at picture C has set her mind up to look for the old woman. The mind, however, cannot see both at once. It can only flip back and forth very quickly.

When a psychologist named R. W. Leeper did this experiment, he found that when subjects were exposed to picture B first, 100 percent perceived the ambiguous picture A as that of a young woman, matching the expectations established by their first having seen picture B. A second group of subjects saw picture C first; 95 percent of these perceived picture A as an old woman, matching the expectations established by their having seen picture C. Expectation is a powerful force in perception.

Now try having your child look at picture E, and ask her what she sees. She will either see a man (left of center) or a rabbit (in the center). Now have her look at picture D, in which the man is much more distinct. Ask her what she sees in picture D. She should see the man clearly. Now have her look back to picture E, and ask her what she sees. The man should "jump out" at her, for the same reasons as those we have seen in the pictures with the old woman/young woman and the dog—mental expectation determines what we see. If your child did not see the rabbit in picture E, tell her there is a rabbit in the picture (or an animal), and see if she can find it. She should be able to, just as she did when you told her there was a dog in the picture in number four.

It's not that seeing isn't believing so much as it is that seeing *can be deceiving* when someone like a psychologist or a magician knows how to fool us.

To your child:

We saw how important making observations in science is—scientists want to see things for themselves. But psychologists—or doctors who study the mind—have shown that seeing can be deceiving. Sometimes things are not as they appear. Let's do some really fun experiments to see if we can fool your eyes and your mind. [Do the experiments.] You see, isn't it strange how one line appears longer than the other line, even when they are the same length. And how one circle appears larger than the other, even though they are the same size. This is because of the other objects in the picture which trick our senses. The small circles around the middle circle make it look larger than the other circle which is surrounded by big circles. This is an optical illusion. Your mind gets set up to expect something, sort of like the hot water/cold water experiment we did.

34. WHAT DO DREAMS MEAN?

To parents: One of the most mysterious and fascinating subjects in all of psychology is the matter of sleep and dreams. Why do we sleep? How much sleep do we need? Why do we dream? What do dreams mean? The famous psychologist Sigmund Freud wrote a well-known book on dreams and how to interpret them; many other psychologists have also studied dreams and tried to understand what they mean. But there's still a lot we don't know about dreams. While psychologists have a number of theories, it's safe to conclude that at this time nobody knows what dreams *really* mean. Dreams are, after all, an individual thing—so the best way to understand what dreams mean is to study your own.

Materials

A small tape recorder

A notebook

Directions: In the first part of this experiment, it might be fun for your child to watch a member of the family sleeping to see when he or she is dreaming. It is actually quite easy to see whether someone is dreaming. You and your child have probably already observed the family dog or cat dreaming—a cat's little paws probably flick and move a bit; a dog will twitch and perhaps make little yelping or barking sounds. People also show dreaming signs. These are called rapid eye movements, or REMs. When someone is dreaming, his eyes, while closed, move very rapidly.

Have your child observe a family member or friend who is sleeping. Before long, this rapid eye movement will be apparent. If it's been arranged with the sleeping family member in advance, awaken him during this phase of sleep and ask him what he was dreaming. He will likely have no trouble in recalling the dream, since it will be fresh on his mind.

In the second part of the experiment, have your child keep track of his dreams from night to night. The best way for him to do this is to have a small tape recorder next to his bed so that when he wakes up during the night or in the morning, he can immediately turn on the tape recorder and describe his dreams. A second option would be for you to ask him to describe his dreams as soon after he awakens as possible. Write the descriptions down for him, keeping a daily record. (You might try doing this yourself, so that you can share your dreams with your child, too.)

After a couple of weeks of recording dreams, help your child to see whether there are any patterns in his dreams. Were they all good dreams or all bad dreams? Were there any nightmares? Did the dreams have something to do with what happened the day before? Who was in the dreams, and what were they doing? Have you or your child learned anything about his hopes or fears by examining his dreams?

Freud believed that dreams act as a passage to the unconscious. Perhaps. If nothing else, they are at least a series of thoughts that occur when we are not trying to think. It's fun to keep track of these thoughts to see whether we can gain any insights into ourselves.

To your child:

Nobody really knows what dreams are for, but psychologists tell us that everyone dreams, and that dreams are very important. Some dreams are about friends, family members, or other people, or about things that have happened to you during the day. Other dreams might be about strange things that didn't really happen. These are fantasy dreams. They help our minds practice imagination. Bad dreams are fantasy dreams, so when you have a bad dream and wake up, just remember that it never really happened and think about good things when you go back to sleep.

Let's watch someone sleeping and see if we can tell when that person is dreaming. [Do the first part of the experiment.] Now let's keep track of your dreams for a couple of weeks and see if we can figure out what they mean. [Do the second part of the experiment.] Since dreams are so personal, only you can really tell what your dreams mean, because they can't mean anything to anyone else. By keeping track of your dreams, you may be able to figure them out.

35. Is There Such a Thing as Luck in Throwing Dice?

To parents: There are two basic "gambler's fallacies" that psychologists discuss: the "lucky streak" fallacy and the "dueness" fallacy. The lucky streak fallacy is when you think you're on a lucky streak of wins and should keep betting as you have been to keep the streak alive. For example, you've thrown several sevens in a row on the dice so you're on a lucky streak. The dueness fallacy is when you've been losing and you're "due" to win. For example, seven hasn't come up in quite some time so it is "due" according to probabilities. The fallacy is that the dice have no memory. They don't know when seven is due. On any given throw of the dice seven has a certain probability of coming up and that probability doesn't change no matter how many sevens have been rolled in the past. In other words, future rolls are not influenced by past rolls. Each roll is independent of the others. To understand how this works, and to demonstrate a few fundamentals of statistics that you and your child will enjoy, the following dice-rolling experiment will show the power of probabilities.

Materials

Graph paper
Pencil
Pair of dice

Directions: Set up a graph similar to the one in Figure 10 with 2 through 12 listed on the horizontal axis. Set it up on the paper vertically to give plenty of room for lots of rolls of the dice. With each roll of the dice, add the two together and mark an "X" above the number on the graph. Keep doing this until the "X's" of one number reach the top of the page. For your child this can be a "race" between the numbers to see which one will get to the top first. Ask him to make a guess which one. He won't know, so begin the experiment and it will become obvious fairly quickly that it will be the 6, 7, or 8. If your dice are "balanced," the 7 should win. Why?

The 7 will win because there are more ways to roll a 7 than any other number. There are six ways to roll a 7, but only five ways to roll a 6 or 8. In fact, as you move away from the number 7

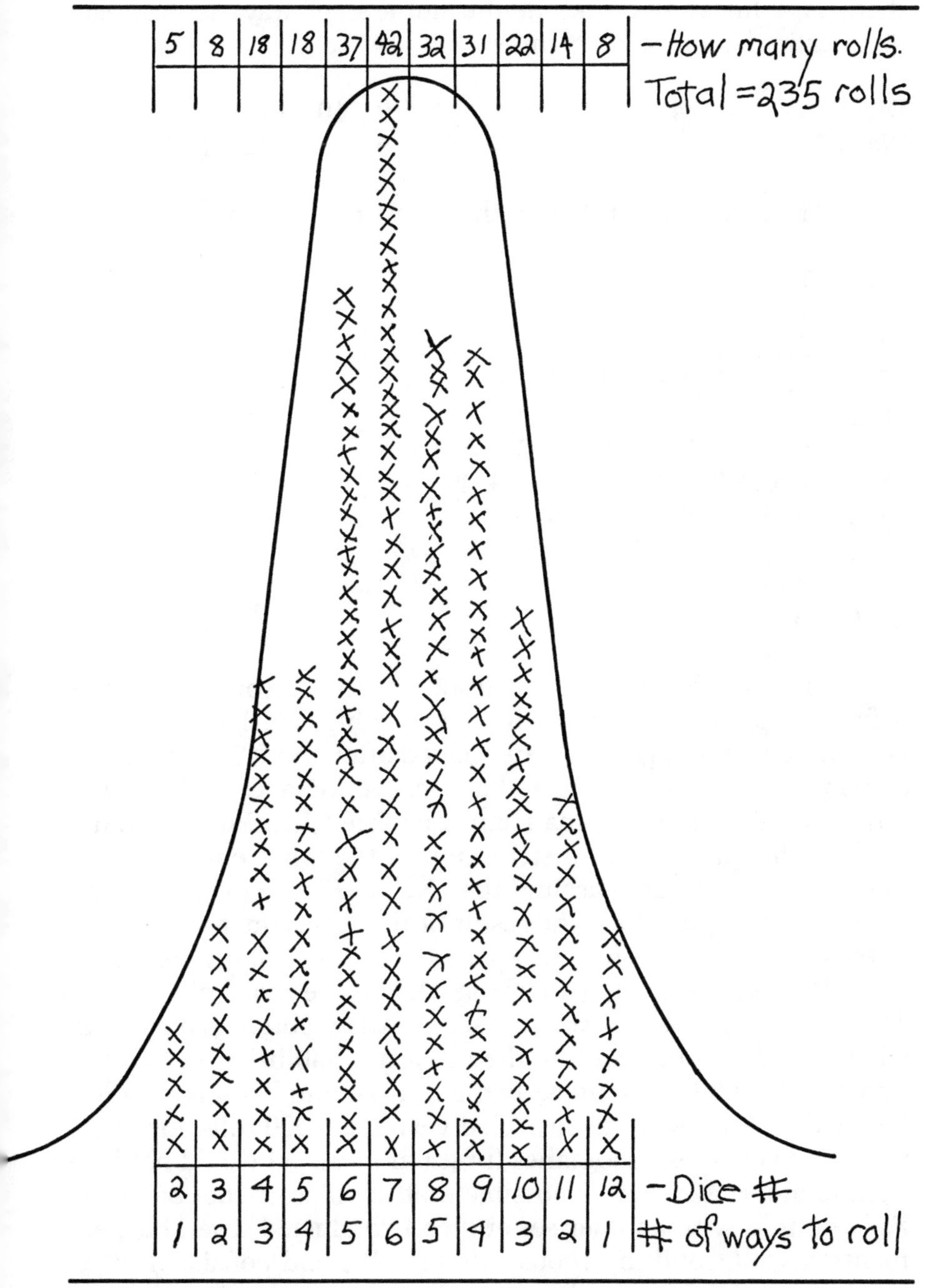

5	8	18	18	37	42	32	31	22	14	8	— How many rolls.

Total = 235 rolls

2	3	4	5	6	7	8	9	10	11	12	— Dice #
1	2	3	4	5	6	5	4	3	2	1	# of ways to roll

FIGURE 10

there is a linear decrease in the number of ways to roll each number in the following manner:

Dice:	2	3	4	5	6	7	8	9	10	11	12
Ways:	1	2	3	4	5	6	5	4	3	2	1

How? The dice can be rolled in the following combinations:

```
 2: 1 + 1
 3: 1 + 2, 2 + 1
 4: 1 + 3, 3 + 1, 2 + 2
 5: 1 + 4, 4 + 1, 2 + 3, 3 + 2
 6: 1 + 5, 5 + 1, 2 + 4, 4 + 2, 3 + 3
 7: 1 + 6, 6 + 1, 2 + 5, 5 + 2, 3 + 4, 4 + 3
 8: 2 + 6, 6 + 2, 3 + 5, 5 + 3, 4 + 4
 9: 3 + 6, 6 + 3, 4 + 5, 5 + 4
10: 4 + 6, 6 + 4, 5 + 5
11: 5 + 6, 6 + 5
12: 6 + 6
```

If you turn the above distribution on its side you will see that it forms a pyramid shape with seven the highest. This, in fact, is how the graph will generally be shaped after about 200 rolls. This distribution is called a bell shape curve, or a Gaussian curve (after the German mathematician Karl Friedrich Gauss, who discovered this principle of distribution in the nineteenth century). I've penciled in a curve around the "X's" in Figure 10 to show this distribution. Figure 10 is the result of this experiment conducted with a six-year-old who did all the marking while I rolled the dice. (He seemed to enjoy marking "X's" more than rolling dice.) The seven "won," but as you can see the distribution is not *exactly* what would be predicted by the above probabilities. In fact, the numbers 6 and 9 are artificially high, while number 4 is a bit low. We made 235 rolls of the dice. Had we made 1,000 rolls, for example, it is likely these anomalies (unusual findings) would not have been found. However, it is possible that the dice are not balanced. For example, with another set of dice I conducted several experiments myself, totalling thousands of rolls, and consistently got the number 8 coming up far more than the number 7. As a scientist I must conclude that there is something wrong with the dice, since the theory predicts something different. This is a case where the theory is not supported by the observations, but we challenge the validity of the observations because they don't match the logical prediction of the theory (which was originally supported with observations with balanced dice that did match the predicted figures).

Paul MacCready gave me the idea for this demonstration. He did this experiment on his own child many years ago and related the story to me of how the morning after he showed his child the experiment, the boy was up at the crack of dawn rolling dice and marking "X's." His son, by the way, eventually went on to become a scientist.

To your child:

In this experiment we're going to have a race with dice. [Set up the graph.] We'll roll the dice and mark an "X" for each number that comes up. Which number do you think will win the race to the top? [He'll respond that he doesn't know.] Let's do the experiment to find out. [About halfway through, or about 100 rolls, ask your child]: If you had $100 to bet on one roll of the dice, which number would you bet would be most likely to come up? [If 7 is "ahead," which it should be, then a quick glance at the graph will give him this answer. If he doesn't see this, point it out.] Let's finish the experiment to see if 7 wins the race to the top. [At the end you can try to explain to him about the different ways to roll each number, but this is a cognitive step that is fairly advanced.] You see, there is really no such thing as luck. Mathematics will predict which numbers will come up, not luck. No matter how many times we do this experiment, the numbers will come up pretty much the same way. This is because of the laws of science that predict with accuracy how the dice will roll.

36. Can You See More Than Meets the Eye?

To parents: If there are any limitations on the power of the mind, these may be as much cognitive as biological. In other words, limitations in thinking may be as much a function of our knowing how to think and what to look for as they are a function of some biological factor that prevents intelligent thinking. Knowing how to think, what to look for, and what questions to ask is half the battle in doing good science or in critical thinking.

Einstein once said that "the answers are there if we can learn to ask the right questions." Often, the limitations on a scientist trying to discover some truth about nature are that he or she isn't asking the right question. If you ask the wrong question, you might get the wrong or useless answer. In this very simple and fun experiment, what will seem like the simplest of questions will turn out to be a "trick" question that can be answered in many different ways: How many squares are there in Figure 10 below?

Materials

The boxes in Figure 11

Directions: Have your child look at Figure 11, and ask her how many squares there are. She will likely get sixteen as the answer. You yourself may have done the same; this is the answer given by most people. But, as you might expect from my introduction to this experiment, this is the wrong answer! There are actually *thirty* squares: There are sixteen little squares (four times four), and there is the *entire figure*, which is also a square and so makes seventeen. In addition, there are nine two-by-two squares, bringing us up to twenty-six, and four three-by-three squares, for a total of thirty!

The mind can see more than meets the eye, if it knows what questions to ask. A little prompting on your part, such as suggesting to your child that she look for the two-by-two and the three-by-three squares, should help her to see the figure differently. There is a powerful message in this experiment, and that is that the mind is much more capable than most of us realize. We all have the capacity to "see" things that we never "saw" before simply by learning to ask different questions and to use different thinking strategies. There is nothing mystical about developing this power. This is what scientists do almost every day. They are trying to think of new ways to see things and of different questions to ask, in order to get new and different answers. This is what the scientific enterprise is all about.

To your child:

How many squares are there in this picture? Let's count them together. That's right, there *are* sixteen. But guess what: there are a lot *more* than sixteen, but these other squares are "hidden." Squares come in all sizes, and

FIGURE 11

there are more than just these little squares [pointing to the smallest squares]. Look, this whole thing is a square, so that makes seventeen. And each of these two-by-two blocks is a square [count all of these and have your child draw them on a photocopy of Figure 11]. And there are these three-by-three squares [count all of these and have your child draw them on the copy of the figure]. So now how many do we have? That's right, thirty squares! Wow!! At first we thought there were only sixteen squares, but now we see that there are actually thirty. Where did they all come from? They were always there. It's just that we needed to look at the figure differently to see more of the squares.

This is what science is all about—learning to look for things that you can't see at first.

EXPERIMENTS AND THE SCIENTIFIC METHOD

As I've tried to demonstrate in this chapter, most principles of science are really quite simple and basic. If the teaching is done correctly, with visual aids and hands-on demonstrations used (three-dimensional science, as I have called it), these principles are readily understandable. To be able to explain them to your child, all you need to do is acquire a few fundamental principles. You can then make the facts and concepts of science come alive for your child, as in the preceding experiments demonstrating Newton's third law (the law of action and reaction) and the concept of light refraction through a prism.

These experiments have done more than just occupy your child's time with fun activities. They were designed to follow the format of the scientific method (chapter 4) as much as possible. If you recall, the fourth step in the scientific method is to conduct an experiment to verify a prediction or hypothesis. Each of the experiments in this chapter has been introduced as a question that we would attempt to answer by conducting the experiment. Within each experiment, the activity itself was carried out to verify or reject a hypothesis implicit within the question. For example: Why are there high and low sounds? Because of fast and slow vibrations. The experiment with the rubber band proved this to be correct. How do we taste food? The answer seems obvious—with our taste buds, of course—right? Wrong. The experiment we did proved that our noses and eyes are also involved in the sense of taste. Conducting experiments is actually playing the game of science. It's one thing to read about science; it's quite another to do it.

Taking a few minutes to teach the basic principles of science to your child also gives you a far more thorough understanding of those principles than you may have had before. On many an occasion, I have been explaining a principle of science to a student or child when, right in the middle of a sentence, a light bulb has appeared in my head—"Aha, *now* I understand that!" Saying the words out loud is very different from just thinking them to yourself. It has the effect of clarifying things in your own mind. One suggestion might be to have your child explain the rules of science, or do some of the experiments with another child. Here the learner becomes the teacher. The reversed roles will reinforce what your child has learned, as well as give him the opportunity to share his newfound knowledge of and excitement for science.

In the next chapter, we will pursue three-dimensional science further and actually see science in action. Here, you will be helping your child move on from learning the fundamentals of doing science to observing how professionals play the game.

CHAPTER

6

Seeing Science in Action

To see science in action and to see others doing science, you will have to take your child to a place where scientists work or where the products of science are on display. Such places as scientific laboratories; colleges and universities; zoos and natural history museums; aquariums; museums of science, industry, and technology; and observatories and planetariums are all great places to take kids for entertainment and education.

A list of nearly every major museum of science and industry, natural history, and the like can be found in Appendix 4, organized by region and state. Nearly every city in America has such places. I've listed all the major ones, but there are many others. One has only to make a few phone calls to find out where and when they are open to the public. In the Los Angeles area (where I live), for example, there are the Jet Propulsion Laboratory, more than a dozen colleges and universities (including Cal Tech and UCLA), the California Museum of Natural History, the California Museum of Science and Industry, the Cabrillo Marine Museum (in San Pedro), Sea World (in San Diego), the Griffith Park Observatory and Planetarium, the Mount Wilson Observatory, the George C. Page Museum and La Brea Tar Pits, the Los Angeles Zoo, the El Dorado Nature Center, the Palm Springs Desert Museum, and so on. Take a look in the Yellow Pages—you'll be surprised at how much science is going on around you.

In addition, check your local newspaper listings for science activities. For example, every Monday the *Los Angeles Times* publishes a "Science/Medicine" section that includes one or two feature articles, a half-dozen science "news briefs," and, most important, a "Science Calendar" listing science activities, displays, lectures, films, television shows, and a "Science for Kids" section.

For example, on December 19, 1988, this section featured an article on robots and news briefs about memory, women teaching medicine, insecticides, and cancer research. The Science Calendar included a description of a hands-on children's tour at the Santa Barbara Museum of Natural History's Sea Center, where kids could participate in "collecting and examining sea creatures." Under "Science for Kids," it was announced that during the Christmas break the El Dorado Nature Center was offering children ages five to nine the opportunity to "learn about whales, reptiles, birds, dinosaurs, and mammals in a series of workshops . . . [aimed at teaching] children about their environment."

Many other major city newspapers now include such sections in their publications. These are good places to start to find out what's happening in the world of science.

WHERE TO FIND SCIENCE IN ACTION

Science Labs

Most publicly funded institutions, such as the Jet Propulsion Laboratory, hold "open houses" for the general public once or twice a year. These are great opportunities for you and your child to see science on the cutting edge. Such institutions typically have hands-on displays for kids, and even the most active of children will be entertained for hours. Also, most universities and colleges have public-speaking programs through which science professors visit grammar schools to lecture on various subjects. These lectures usually include a multitude of visual aids.

Museums

Where museums of natural history and of science, industry, and technology were in the past dull and dusty places for the unusually curious only, today they are typically designed to be hands-on, interactive, exciting places for visitors of all ages. I've had the opportunity to visit most of the major science and natural history museums in the United States, and I've noticed the transition that has been taking place over the past ten years. There are now buttons to push, levers to pull, lights, sounds, charts, and graphs—a Rube Goldberg delight! A visit to a modern museum is a sensory experience that even the most uninterested of children will find compelling.

The Natural History Museum of Los Angeles, for example, used to be a collection of old bones and stuffed animals, with layers of dust on the displays in the corners. I remember as a six-year-old visiting the dinosaur rooms and being overwhelmed by their size and their ominous teeth. I was curious and impressed, but I wasn't excited. It wasn't a *fun* place to go. And even though today I teach a course in evolution, I always preferred the Museum of Science and Industry over the Natural History Museum, because there were more things to do there; it was far more stimulating.

Today, the Natural History Museum is alive with interactive displays and beautiful exhibits. The museum has added a children's "petting" room, so that instead of seeing those great dinosaur bones behind Plexiglas and giant signs saying KEEP HANDS OFF, kids can actually pick the bones up and hold them. At the museum you can run your hand over a leopard skin, touch a shark's teeth, feel the shell of a giant tortoise, and look at and touch hundreds of types of bird feathers, snakeskins, mammal furs, and so on. Such experiences make science come alive in the third dimension for your child.

Most museums are now moving toward three-dimensional science. For example, the Cabrillo Marine Museum in San Pedro, California, along with most marine museums around the country, has a "petting" display for children so that they can actually hold various tide-pool beasties, such as starfishes, sea cucumbers, octopi, sea urchins, and the like. When I take the college students from my evolution class there, we stand around the tank—college students next to five- and six-year-olds—all equally awed by the beauty and wonder of nature's diversity.

At many natural history museums, such as the George C. Page Museum and La Brea Tar Pits, you can actually see paleontologists (those who study fossils) at work through a large Plexiglas window. Small signs explain what they are doing. And *all* museums, with advance notice, have special programs, tours, and films for groups of children. Museum guides work with kids every day, and they have experience in keeping a large group entertained.

Many cities also have specialty museums, which are usually listed in city guidebooks and in the Yellow Pages. For example, The Pima Air Museum in Tucson, Arizona, has hundreds of planes and jets that visitors are allowed to explore, and the B-52 bomber graveyard next door to the museum is a sight to behold. The Monterey Bay Aquarium in Monterey, California, is purported to have the finest display of aquatic creatures in the world. Ripley's "Believe It or Not" Museum in San Francisco is filled with items of all sorts that are, well, hard to believe—but very entertaining. And the Smithsonian Institution museums in Washington, D.C.— particularly the National Air and Space Museum—are, of course, without parallel.

To see the real thing in space history, there is nothing more impressive than taking a trip to Cape Canaveral in Florida, where you and your child can see an actual-size replica of the Saturn V rocket that went to the moon, lying on its side.

Observatories and Planetariums

Observatories and planetariums have numerous things to do that are both entertaining and educational. It's a wonderful thrill for anyone, and especially for a child, to take a first look through a giant telescope and see the craters of the moon, the rings of Saturn, or the moons of Jupiter.

There are usually displays that show the sizes of the planets relative to one another and to the sun. Special scales show you what you would weigh on the moon, Mars, Venus, Jupiter, or Pluto, dramatically demonstrating the varying effects of gravity based on the sizes of the planets. A solar telescope reveals sunspots. A giant glass globe, when touched, causes your hair to stand on end, showing the effects of wireless electricity in the air.

The planetarium—a large dome with a giant ball-shaped projector in the middle—reveals the night sky with a brilliance and clarity you could never experience in a city, with its obscuring light pollution. When I began to study astronomy in my freshman year in college, I took my six-year-old sister, Tina, to the Griffith

Park Observatory. I'll never forget her incredulity as the lights went down and the night sky was projected onto the dome. "We're outside!" she exclaimed, rather loudly.

The projections *are* very realistic, and they have the added advantage of allowing the speaker to use a light pointer, constellation patterns, and the like to turn the night sky into a teaching tool. I once gave a lecture at the Griffith Park Observatory on the origins of life and the possibilities of extraterrestrial intelligence, and I found that working the hundreds of switches, knobs, and controls behind the lectern was really a thrill. It was the ultimate video game, and the greatest teaching tool/visual aid I'd ever used. The programs are inexpensive (free for young children), and even if your child doesn't understand everything going on, a planetarium show is one of the sensory experiences of a lifetime.

If the planetarium or science and industry museum in your area has an IMAX or OMNIMAX theater, this too is a must-see for the entire family. The movies are projected onto a giant screen, 100 feet high, and the audience is enveloped in sights and sounds. The films (on flying, spaceflight, rafting trips down the Colorado River in the Grand Canyon, and so on) are extremely realistic. The thrill of watching the launch of the space shuttle as if you were really there in Florida is incomparable.

Science Classes

Many museums offer classes in science for children that meet after school, on Saturdays, or during vacations. For instance, the California Museum of Science and Industry recently began a series of classes entitled "The Gift of Science: Science Workshops for Children." The program offers a variety of classes for children, ranging in levels from preschool to eighth grade. Classes meet on Saturdays for two to four hours. The program cost ranges from $15 to $65, with scholarships offered to children of needy families. The classes cover a variety of subjects, including weather, music, aerospace, rocketry, mathematics, dinosaurs, electricity, photography, whales, and so on. In the four-week rocketry class, for example, the children are taught the principles of rocketry, space flight, and rocket construction. By the final day they have completed building their own rockets, which they then fly!

When appropriate, the children are also allowed to use the museum facilities, teaching tools, and science displays for more in-depth understanding. Last year, preschoolers could learn about dinosaurs and whales while their older brothers and sisters took classes with such names as "Ice Cream for Science," "Junior Astronauts," and "Pythons to Pollywogs." Such classes offer a wonderful opportunity for learning, and they are now becoming available at many other such institutions.

WHAT NEXT?

You've taught your child how to think scientifically, how to tell the difference between science and pseudoscience, what some of the rules of the game of science are, how science is actually done, and where to see science in action. What's next? This book is just the first, tiny step on a long journey into the fascinating world of science for you and your child. The appendices that follow provide information on books and magazines on science for you and your child, as well as a list of science museums across the country. A list of easy-to-acquire materials for creating a science "tool kit" is also provided. You can use such a kit in an infinite variety of ways to teach your child the basic principles of science. Also included is a listing of scientific companies to which you can write for free or inexpensive scientific equipment or information. Finally, a "map" of the sciences is provided to help you and your child determine where his or her main interests lie. You can then look in the encyclopedia and go to the library to get more information on any area of science your child is interested in pursuing further. This listing consists of virtually every branch of science there is; from here, the door is wide open.

I invite you and your child to pick one or more of the sciences and explore to your hearts' content, remembering what the great nineteenth-century naturalist, science popularizer, essayist, and teacher Thomas Henry Huxley wrote:

> Sit down before a fact as a little child, be prepared to give up every preconceived notion, follow humbly wherever and to whatever abyss nature leads, or you shall learn nothing.

APPENDIX

1

Books on Science for Parents
AN ANNOTATED BIBLIOGRAPHY

Abbott, Edwin. 1963. *Flatland.* New York: Barnes & Noble. A delightful romp through the world of two dimensions.

Abell, George, and Barry Singer. 1981. *Science and the Paranormal.* New York: Charles Scribner's Sons. A collection of essays by noted scientists such as Carl Sagan and Isaac Asimov about UFOs, pyramid power, psychic healing, the Bermuda Triangle, biorhythms, life after death, and other topics.

Anderson, Ronald, et al. 1970. *Developing Children's Thinking through Science.* Englewood Cliffs, N. J.: Prentice-Hall.

Boorstin, Daniel. 1983. *The Discoverers.* New York: Random House. The author, a scholarly historian, has written a classic for the uninitiated about the history of great discoveries. Highly readable.

Brandes, Louis. 1979. *Science Can Be Fun.* Portland, Maine: J. Weston Walch.

Bronowski, J. 1965. *Science and Human Values.* New York: Harper & Row. A mathematician looks at the human side of science.

_____. 1973. *The Ascent of Man.* Boston: Little, Brown & Co. The book that accompanied the award-winning television show of the same name.

Burke, James. 1978. *Connections.* Boston: Little, Brown & Co. A television documentary producer looks at the unusual connections among science, technology, and society.

118

————. 1985. *The Day the Universe Changed*. Boston: Little, Brown & Co. The ten most important events in the history of science come alive in this companion to the television series of the same name.

Butts, David. 1975. *Children and Science: The Process of Teaching and Learning*. Englewood Cliffs, N. J.: Prentice-Hall.

Carin, Arthur, and Robert Sund. 1975. *Teaching Science through Discovery*. Columbus: Charles E. Merrill Publishing Co.

Dethier, Vincent. 1962. *To Know a Fly*. New York: Holden-Day. A biologist writes for the general public on the romance of, and reasons for, being a scientist.

Epstein, Lewis. 1988. *Thinking Physics*. San Francisco: Insight Press. An excellent question-and-answer approach to physics that's great for helping parents to answer children's questions or for making a game of raising the questions and then answering them. "Epstein's Law" is that "there is an easy way to explain anything."

Friedl, Alfred. 1972. *Teaching Science to Children: The Inquiry Approach Applied*. New York: Random House.

Gardner, Martin. 1957. *Fads and Fallacies in the Name of Science*. New York: Dover Publications. A science popularizer shows us what *isn't* science.

————. 1981. *Science: Good, Bad and Bogus*. Buffalo, N.Y.: Prometheus Books. A joyful collection of essays on a skeptical and scientific examination of claims of the paranormal.

Good, Ronald G. 1977. *How Children Learn Science*. New York: Macmillan.

Gould, Stephen Jay. 1982. *The Panda's Thumb*. New York: W. W. Norton. The finest biology popularizer in America makes evolution come to life.

Greenler, Robert. 1980. *Rainbows, Halos, and Glories*. London: Cambridge University Press. A readable and practical guide to explain atmospheric phenomena.

Hardison, Richard. 1988. *Upon the Shoulders of Giants*. New York: University Press of America. A highly readable, very stimulating history of the most important ideas that have shaped the modern mind.

Hellemans, Alexander, and Bryan Bunch. 1988. *The Timetables of Science: A Chronology of the Most Important People and Events in the History of Science*. New York: Simon & Schuster.

Hubler, H. Clark. 1974. *Science for Children*. New York: Random House.

Lowery, Lawrence F. 1978. *The Everyday Science Sourcebook*. Boston: Allyn & Bacon.

McCain, G., and E. M. Segal. 1969. *The Game of Science.* Monterey, Calif.: Brooks/Cole Publishing Company. A good introduction to the basics of science that makes science fun.

Minnaert, M. 1954. *The Nature of Light and Colour in the Open Air.* New York: Dover. Scientific explanations for atmospheric phenomena.

Moore, Shirley. 1960. *Science Projects Handbook.* Washington, D.C.: Science Service.

Munson, Howard R. 1962. *Science Activities with Simple Things.* Belmont, Calif.: Fearon Pitman Publishers.

Olson, Richard. 1982. *Science Deified and Science Defied.* Berkeley, Calif.: University of California Press. A thorough history of the development of science through the ages.

Randi, James. 1982. *Flim-Flam!* Buffalo, N.Y.: Prometheus Books. Magician/scientist James "The Amazing" Randi exposes frauds and tricksters who use science to deceive.

Sagan, Carl. 1979. *Broca's Brain.* New York: Random House. The world's most famous scientist shows the public the importance of science in our culture through this collection of essays.

———. 1980. *Cosmos.* New York: Random House. The companion book to the most-watched documentary science series ever.

Schatz, Albert. 1971. *Teaching Science with Garbage.* Emmaus, Pa.: Rodale Press.

Scott, John M. 1970. *The Everyday Living Approach to Teaching Elementary Science.* West Nyack, N.Y.: Parker Publishing Co.

Stone, A. Harris, Fred Geis, and Louis Kuslan. 1971. *Experiences for Teaching Children Science.* Belmont, Calif.: Wadsworth.

Strongin, Herb. 1976. *Science on a Shoestring.* Reading, Mass.: Addison-Wesley.

Sund, Robert, William Tillery, and Leslie Trowbridge. 1975. *Investigate and Discover: Elementary Science Lessons.* Boston: Allyn & Bacon.

Trojack, Doris A. 1979. *Science with Children.* New York: McGraw-Hill.

UNESCO. 1962. *700 Science Experiments for Everyone.* Garden City, N.Y.: Doubleday & Co.

———. 1976. *New UNESCO Sourcebook for Science Teaching.* New York: UNIPUB.

Viorst, Judith. 1971. *150 Science Experiments Step-by-Step.* New York: Bantam Books.

Wood, Elizabeth. 1975. *Science from Your Airplane Window.* New York: Dover. Principles of scientific observing are well explored in this fun book that will enlighten your next flight.

Books on Science
for Children
(With a Little Help from Their Parents)

Blackwelder, Sheila. 1980. *Science for All Seasons.* Englewood Cliffs, N.J.: Prentice-Hall. Science experiences and experiments for young children for every season of the year.

Broekel, Ray. 1983. *Sound Experiments.* Chicago: Children's Press/A New True Book. Pictures and guides to simple experiments. See the collection of New True Books for children.

————. 1986. *Experiments with Light.* Chicago: Children's Press/A New True Book.

Caras, R. 1975. *A Zoo in Your Room.* New York: Harcourt Brace Jovanovich.

Cobb, Vicki. 1972. *Science Experiments You Can Eat.* New York: Harper & Row. How to turn your kitchen into a laboratory.

Cobb, Vicki, and Kathy Darling. 1980. *Bet You Can't!—Science Impossibilities to Fool You.* New York: Lothrop, Lee & Shepard.

Discovery Center of Science and Technology. 1987. *Science Soup.* Syracuse, N.Y.: Discovery Center of Science and Technology. According to the book's subtitle—*Science You Can Cook Up at Home*— this tells you how to perform inexpensive and practical scientific experiments in the kitchen.

Gardner, Martin. 1981. *Entertaining Science Experiments with Everyday Objects.* New York: Dover.

Gardner, Robert. 1986. *Ideas for Science Projects.* New York: Franklin Watts. A collection of simple and effective science experiments that parents and teachers can do with children.

Holt, Bess-Gene. 1977. *Science with Young Children.* Washington, D.C.: National Association for the Education of Young Children. An excellent resource book on what every parent and teacher should know about science education for young children.

Hays, Kim, ed. 1984. *T.V., Science and Kids: Teaching Our Children to Question.* Reading, Mass.: Addison-Wesley. A collection of essays by scientists and educators on using television productively.

McGavack, J., Jr., and D. P. La Salle. 1969. *Guppies, Bubbles, and Vibrating Objects.* New York: John Day.

Medawar, Peter. 1979. *Advice to a Young Scientist.* New York: Harper & Row.

Milgrom, Harry. 1970. *ABC Science Experiments.* New York: Macmillan.

Schmidt, V. T., and V. N. Rockcastle. 1968. *Teaching Science with Everyday Things.* New York: McGraw-Hill.

Wood, Elizabeth. 1975. *Science from Your Airplane Window.* New York: Dover.

Periodicals for Parents and Children

Appraisal: Science Books for Young Children. 3 issues per year. Children's Science Book Review Committee, 36 Cummington St., Boston, MA 02215. Reviews of science books for children.

Chickadee. 10 issues per year. Young Naturalist Foundation, P.O. Box 11314, Des Moines, IA 50340. Information and activities for children about nature.

Discover: The Newsmagazine of Science. Monthly. Time-Life Building, 541 N. Fairbanks Court, Chicago, IL 60611. An illustrated magazine of popularized science for the general public.

Electric Company. 10 issues per year. Children's Television Workshop, One Lincoln Plaza, New York, NY 10023. A thematic approach gives children different activities to explore each month.

National Geographic World. Monthly. National Geographic Society, 17th and M Sts., NW, Washington, DC 20036. A natural history magazine for children.

Odyssey: Young People's Magazine of Astronomy and Outer Space. Monthly. Astromedia Corp., 625 E. St. Paul Ave., Milwaukee, WI 53202. Well-illustrated information on science, space, and astronomy for children.

Owl. 10 issues per year. Young Naturalist Foundation, P.O. Box 11314, Des Moines, IA 50304. A magazine for children's inquiring minds about science and nature. Develops a thirst for wonder.

Ranger Rick's Nature Magazine. Monthly. National Wildlife Federation, 1412 16th St., NW, Washington, DC 20036. An illustrated ecology magazine for children ages five to twelve.

Science and Children. 8 issues per year. National Science Teachers Association, 1742 Connecticut Ave., NW, Washington, DC 20009. Illustrated ideas about teaching children science, for elementary and junior-high-school science teachers.

Science Weekly. 18 issues per year. *Science Weekly,* P.O. Box 70154, Washington, DC 20088–0154. Using a thematic approach, each issue deals with a specific topic in science, math, and technology. Included are teaching notes for parents, a bibliography for further exploration of a topic, questions to ask your child about the subject covered, and hands-on activities to help your child learn about a particular science.

Scienceland. 8 issues per year. Scienceland, Inc., 501 Fifth Ave, New York, NY 10017–6165. Color photographs and excellent illustrations bring to life the world of science and nature for your child. Each issue focuses on a particular subject, such as space, pill bugs, etc.

Your Big Backyard. Monthly. National Wildlife Federation, 1412 16th St., NW, Washington, DC 20036–2266. Simple text and photos to help young children learn about science.

Zoobooks. 10 issues per year. Wildlife Education, Ltd., 930 West Washington St., San Diego, CA 92103. Each issue focuses on a particular animal or species, with color photos and simple text.

3-2-1 Contact. 10 issues per year. Children's Television Workshop, P.O. Box 2933, Boulder, CO 80321. A science magazine for young children, based on the television series of the same name.

4

Science and Nature Museums, by Region and State

SOUTHWEST

Arizona

Arizona Museum of Science and Technology
 80 N. Second St., Phoenix, AZ 85004; 602/256-9388
Arizona-Sonora Desert Museum
 2021 N. Kinney Rd., Tucson, AZ 85743; 602/883-1380
Center for Meteorite Studies
 Arizona State University, Tempe, AZ 85187; 602/965-6511
Tucson Children's Museum
 300 East University Blvd., Tucson, AZ 85705; 602/884-7511

California

Bowers Museum
 2002 N. Main St., Santa Ana, CA 92706; 714/972-1900
Cabrillo Marine Museum
 3720 Stephen White Dr., San Pedro, CA 90731; 213/548-7563
California Academy of Science
 Golden Gate Park, San Francisco, CA 94118; 415/221-5100
California Museum of Science and Industry
 700 State Dr., Los Angeles, CA 90037; 213/744-7400
Diablo Valley College Museum
 Golf Club Rd., Pleasant Hills, CA 94523; 415/685-1230

The Discovery Center
1944 N. Winery Ave., Fresno, CA 93703; 209/251-5533

The Exploratorium
3601 Lyon St., San Francisco, CA 94123; 415/563-7337

Griffith Park Observatory
2800 E. Observatory Rd., Los Angeles, CA 90028; 213/664-1191

Lawrence Hall of Science
University of California, Berkeley, CA 94720; 415/642-5133

Marine World Africa USA
Marine World Parkway, Vallejo, CA 94589; 707/644-4000

Reuben H. Fleet Space Theater and Science Center
1875 El Prado, Balboa Park, San Diego, CA 92103; 619/238-1233

Sacramento Science Center and Junior Museum
3615 Auburn Blvd., Sacramento, CA 95821; 916/449-8255

Santa Barbara Museum of Natural History
2559 Puesta del Sol Rd., Santa Barbara, CA 93105; 805/682-4711

Scripps Aquarium—Museum/Scripps Institution of Oceanography
8602 La Jolla Shores Dr., La Jolla, CA 92093; 619/534-6804

Sea World, Inc.
1720 South Shores Rd., San Diego, CA 92109; 619/222-6363

Zoological Society of San Diego/San Diego Zoo
and Wild Animal Park
P.O. Box 551, San Diego, CA 92112; 619/231-1515

Colorado

Denver Museum of Natural History/The Hall of Life
2001 Colorado Blvd., Denver, CO 80206; 719/376-6423

Hawaii

The Bishop Museum
1525 Bernice St., Honolulu, HI 96817; 808/847-3511

New Mexico

Museum of New Mexico
113 Lincoln Ave., Santa Fe, NM 87503; 505/827-6450

New Mexico Museum of Natural History
P.O. Box 7010, Albuquerque, NM 87194; 505/841-8837

Utah

Children's Museum of Utah
840 N. 300 West, Salt Lake City, UT 84103; 801/328-3383

Hansen Planetarium
15 South State St., Salt Lake City, UT 84111; 801/538-2104

NORTHWEST

Oregon

Oregon Museum of Science and Industry
  4015 SW Canyon Rd., Portland, OR 97221; 503/222-2828
Willamette Science and Technology Center
  2300 Centennial Blvd., Eugene, OR 97440; 206/325-4510

Washington

Hanford Science Center
  825 Jadwin Ave., Box 1970, Mail Stop A1-60, Richland, WA 99352;
  509/376-6374
Pacific Science Center
  200 Second Ave. N., Seattle, WA 98109; 206/443-2001
The Seattle Aquarium
  Pier 59, Waterfront Park, Seattle, WA 98101; 206/625-5015
Washington Park Arboretum/Center for Urban Horticulture
  University of Washington, XD-10, Seattle, WA 98195; 206/325-4510

MIDWEST

Illinois

Center for American Archeology
  P.O. Box 366, Kampsville, IL 62050; 618/653-4316
Chicago Zoological Park
  8400 West 31st St., Brookfield, IL 60513; 312/485-0263
Field Museum of Natural History
  Roosevelt Rd. at Lake Shore Dr., Chicago, IL 60605; 312/922-9410
John G. Shedd Aquarium
  1200 South Lake Shore Dr., Chicago, IL 60605; 312/939-2426
Lakeview Museum of the Arts and Sciences
  1125 West Lake Ave., Peoria, IL 61614; 309/686-7000
Lincoln Park Zoological Garden
  2200 N. Cannon Dr., Chicago, IL 60614; 312/294-4660
Museum of Science and Industry
  57th & Lake Shore Dr., Chicago, IL 60637; 312/684-1414
Museum of the Chicago Academy of Sciences
  2001 N. Clark St., Chicago, IL 60614; 312/549-0606

Indiana

The Children's Museum, Indianapolis
  P.O. Box 3000, Indianapolis, IN 46206; 317/924-5431

Evansville Museum of Arts and Sciences
411 S.E. Riverside Dr., Evansville, IN 47713; 812/425-2406

Michigan

Children's Museum, Detroit Public Schools
67 East Kirby, Detroit, MI 48202; 313/494-1210
Cranbrook Institute of Science
500 Lone Pine Rd., Bloomfield Hills, MI 48013; 313/645-3261
Detroit Science Center
5020 John R. St., Detroit, MI 48202; 313/577-8400
Impression 5 Science Museum
200 Museum Dr., Lansing, MI 48933; 517/485-8116
Michigan Space Center
2111 Emmons Rd., Jackson, MI 49201; 517/787-4425
The Michigan State University Museum
West Circle Dr., East Lansing, MI 48824; 517/355-2370

Ohio

Cincinnati Museum of Natural History
1720 Gilbert Ave., Cincinnati, OH 45202; 513/621-3889
Cleveland Children's Museum
10730 Euclid Ave., Cleveland, OH 44106; 216/791-7114
Cleveland Health Education Museum
8911 Euclid Ave., Cleveland, OH 44106; 216/231-5010
Ohio's Center of Science and Industry
280 E. Broad St., Columbus, OH 43215; 614/228-5619

Wisconsin

Discovery World Museum of Science, Economics and Technology
818 West Wisconsin Ave., Milwaukee, WI 53233; 414/765-9966
Milwaukee Public Museum
800 W. Wells St., Milwaukee, WI 53233; 414/278-2700

NORTH CENTRAL

Iowa

The Science Center of Iowa
4500 Grand Ave., Des Moines, IA 50312; 515/274-4138

Kansas

Kansas Learning Center for Health
309 Main St., Halstead, KS 67056; 316/835-2662
University of Kansas Museum of Natural History
University of Kansas, Lawrence, KS 66045; 913/864-4541

Minnesota

James Ford Bell Museum of Natural History
   10 Church St., SE, Minneapolis, MN 55455; 612/624-1852
The Mayo Medical Museum
   Mayo Clinic, 200 First St., SW, Rochester, MN 55901; 507/284-3280
Science Museum of Minnesota
   30 East 10th St., St. Paul, MN 55101; 612/221-9410

Missouri

The Kansas City Museum
   3218 Gladstone Blvd., Kansas City, MO 64123; 816/483-8300
The Magic House/St. Louis Children's Museum
   516 S. Kirkwood Rd., St. Louis, MO 63122; 314/822-8900
Missouri Botanical Garden
   P.O. Box 299, St. Louis, MO 63166; 314/577-5100
St. Louis Science Center and Science Park
   Forest Park, 5050 Oakland Ave., St. Louis, MO 63110; 314/289-4400

Nebraska

Fontenelle Forest Nature Center
   1111 Bellevue Blvd. N., Bellevue, NE 68005; 402/731-3140
University of Nebraska State Museum of Natural Science
   212 Morrill Hall, 14th & U Sts., Lincoln, NE 68588; 402/472-2637

South Dakota

Badlands National Park
   Box 6, Cedar Pass, SH240, Interior, SD 57750; 605/433-5361

SOUTH CENTRAL

Arkansas

Arkansas Museum of Science and History
   MacArthur Park, Little Rock, AR 72202; 501/371-3521

Louisiana

Audubon Park and Zoological Garden
   6500 Magazine St., Audubon Park, New Orleans, LA 70178;
   504/861-2537
Louisiana Nature and Science Center
   11000 Lake Forest Blvd., New Orleans, LA 70127; 504/241-9606
LSU Museum of Geoscience
   Howe-Russell Geoscience Complex, Room 135, Louisiana State University, Baton Rouge, LA 70803; 504/388-2296

Oklahoma

Kirkpatrick Center Museum Complex
  2100 Northeast 52nd, Oklahoma City, OK 73111; 405/427-5461
Omniplex Science Museum
  2100 N.E. 52nd St., Oklahoma City, OK 73111; 405/424-5545

Texas

Dallas Museum of Natural History/Dallas Aquarium
  P.O. Box 26193, Fair Park Station, Dallas, TX 75226; 214/670-8460
Don Harrington Discovery Center
  1200 Streit Dr., Amarillo, TX 79106; 806/255-9547
Fort Worth Museum of Science and History
  1501 Montgomery St., Ft. Worth, TX 76107; 817/732-1631
Houston Museum of Medical Science
  1 Herman Circle Dr., Houston, TX 77030; 713/529-3766
Insights—El Paso Science Museum
  303 N. Oregon St., El Paso, TX 79901; 915/542-2990
The Science Place
  P.O. Box 11158, Fair Park, Dallas, TX 75223; 214/428-7200
Strecker Museum
  South 4th St., Baylor University, Waco, TX 76798; 817/755-1110

NORTHEAST

Connecticut

Lutz Children's Museum
  247 South Main St., Manchester, CT 06040; 203/643-0949
Museum of Art, Science, and Industry
  4450 Park Ave., Bridgeport, CT 06604; 203/372-3521
Mystic Marinelife Aquarium
  55 Coogan Blvd., Mystic, CT 06355; 203/536-9631
Science Museum of Connecticut
  950 Trout Brook Dr., West Hartford, CT 06119; 203/236-2961
Thames Science Center
  Gallows Lane, New London, CT 06320; 203/442-0391

Maine

Department of Marine Resources
  State House Station #21, Augusta, ME 04333; 207/289-2099
State of Maine Marine Resources Laboratory
  McKown Point, West Boothbay Harbor, ME 04575; 207/633-5572

Maryland

Calvert Marine Museum
P.O. Box 97, Solomons, MD 20688; 301/326-2042

Howard B. Owens Science Center
9601 Greenbelt Rd., Lanham, MD 20706; 301/577-8718

Maryland Academy of Sciences/Maryland Science Center
601 Light St., Baltimore, MD 21230; 301/685-2370

National Aquarium in Baltimore
501 East Pratt St., Pier 3, Baltimore, MD 21202; 301/576-3800

Massachusetts

The Children's Museum
Museum Wharf, 300 Congress St., Boston, MA 02210; 617/426-6500

The Computer Museum
Museum Wharf, 300 Congress St., Boston, MA 02210; 617/426-2800

The Harvard University Museums
24 Oxford St., Cambridge, MA 02138; 617/495-1000

Museum of Science, Boston
Science Park, Boston, MA 02114; 617/589-0100

National Marine Fisheries Service Aquarium
Woods Hole, MA 02543; 617/548-7684

New England Aquarium
Central Wharf, Boston, MA 02110; 617/973-5200

Springfield Science Museum
236 State St., Springfield, MA 01103; 413/733-1194

New Jersey

Monmouth Museum
Newman Springs Rd., P.O. Box 359, Lincroft, NJ 07738; 201/747-2266

Space Studies Institute
P.O. Box 82, Princeton, NJ 08540; 609/921-0377

New York

Alley Pond Environmental Center, Inc.
228–06 Northern Blvd., Douglaston, NY 11363; 718/229-4000

American Museum of Natural History/Hayden Planetarium
Central Park West at 79th St., New York, NY 10024; 212/769-5000

Aquarium of Niagara Falls
701 Whirlpool St., Niagara Falls, NY 14301; 716/285-3575

Brookhaven National Laboratory, Exhibit Center–Science Museum
Upton, NY 11973; 516/282-4049

Brooklyn Botanical Garden
1000 Washington Ave., Brooklyn, NY 11225; 718/622-4433
Buffalo Museum of Science
Humboldt Pkwy., Buffalo, NY 14211; 716/896-5200
Discovery Center of Science & Technology
321 South Clinton St., Syracuse, NY 13202; 315/425-9068
Museum of Holography
11 Mercer St., New York, NY 10013; 212/925-0581
New York Aquarium
Boardwalk & West 8th St., Brooklyn, NY 11224; 718/265-3400
New York Hall of Science
P.O. Box 1032, 47−01 111th St., Corona, NY 11368; 718/699-0005
New York Zoological Society−Bronx Zoo
Bronx, NY 10460; 212/220-5131
Roberson Center for the Arts and Sciences
30 Front St., Binghamton, NY 13905; 607/772-0660
Schenectady Museum
2500 W. Broad St., Schenectady, NY 12308; 804/367-1013
Science Museum of Long Island
1526 N. Plandome Rd., Manhasset, NY 11030; 516/627-9400

Pennsylvania

The Academy of Natural Sciences of Philadelphia
19th & Benjamin Franklin Pkwy., Philadelphia, PA 19103;
215/299-1100
Buhl Science Center
Allegheny Square, Pittsburgh, PA 15212; 412/321-4302
The Carnegie Museum of Natural History
4400 Forbes Ave., Pittsburgh, PA 15213; 412/622-3131
*Franklin Institute Science Museum and Planetarium
and the Museum-to-Go Resource Center*
20th & Benjamin Franklin Pkwy., Philadelphia, PA 19103;
215/488-1200
Hunt Institute for Botanical Documentation
Carnegie-Mellon University, Pittsburgh, PA 15213; 412/268-2434
Reading Public Museum and Art Gallery
500 Museum Rd., Reading, PA 19611; 215/371-5850

Vermont

Fairbanks Museum and Planetarium
Main & Prospect Sts., St. Johnsbury, VT 05819; 802/748-2372

SOUTHEAST

Alabama

Anniston Museum of Natural History
P.O. Box 1587, Anniston, AL 36202; 205/237-6766

The Discovery Place
1320 33rd St. South, Birmingham, AL 35205; 205/939-1176

Red Mountain Museum
1421 22nd St. South, Birmingham, AL 35205; 205/933-4152

Florida

The Discovery Center
231 Southwest 2nd Ave., Ft. Lauderdale, FL 33301; 305/462-4116

John Young Museum and Planetarium/Orlando Science Center
810 East Rollins St., Orlando, FL 32803; 305/896-7151

Metrozoo
12400 S.W. 152nd St., Miami, FL 22177; 305/251-0401

Miami Seaquarium
4400 Rickenbacker Causeway, Miami, FL 33149; 305/361-5705

Museum of Arts and Science
1040 Museum Blvd., Daytona Beach, FL 32014; 904/255-0285

Museum of Science and Industry
4801 East Fowler Ave., Tampa, FL 33617; 813/985-5531

Museum of Science and Space Transit Planetarium
3280 South Miami Ave., Miami, FL 33129; 305/854-4247

Planet Ocean
The International Oceanographic Foundation, 3979 Rickenbacker
Causeway, Miami, FL 33149; 305/361-5786

The South Florida Science Museum
4801 Dreher Trail N., West Palm Beach, FL 33405; 305/832-2026

Georgia

Fernbank Science Center
156 Heaton Park Dr., NE, Atlanta, GA 30307; 404/378-4311

Museum of Arts and Sciences
4182 Forsyth Rd., Macon, GA 31210; 912/477-3232

Kentucky

The Living Arts and Science Center, Inc.
362 Walnut St., Lexington, KY 40508; 606/252-5222

Museum of History and Science
727 West Main St., Louisville, KY 40202; 502/589-4584

Mississippi

Gulf Coast Research Laboratory/J. L. Scott Marine Education Center
P.O. Box 7000, Ocean Springs, MS 39564; 601/374-5550

Mississippi Museum of Natural Science
111 N. Jefferson St., Jackson, MS 39202; 601/354-7303

North Carolina

The Health Adventure
501 Biltmore Ave., Asheville, NC 28801; 704/254-6373

Nature Science Center
Museum Dr., Winston-Salem, NC 27105; 919/767-6730

North Carolina Aquarium, Fort Fisher
P.O. Box 130, Kure Beach, NC 28449; 919/458-8257

North Carolina Department of Agriculture—North Carolina Maritime Museum
315 Front St., Beaufort, NC 28516; 919/728-7317

North Carolina Museum of Life and Science
433 Murray Ave., Durham, NC 27704; 919/477-0431

Science Museums of Charlotte, Inc./Nature Museum/Discovery Place
301 North Tryon St., Charlotte, NC 29202; 704/372-6262

South Carolina

The Charleston Museum
360 Meeting St., Charleston, SC 29403; 803/722-2996

Roper Mountain Science Center
504 Roper Mountain Rd., Greenville, SC 29615; 803/297-0232

Tennessee

American Museum of Science & Energy
300 South Tulane Ave., Oak Ridge, TN 37830; 615/576-3200

Cumberland Science Museum
800 Ridley Rd., Nashville, TN 37203; 615/259-6099

Memphis Pink Palace Museum and Planetarium
3050 Central Ave., Memphis, TN 38111; 901/454-5603

Virginia

Science Museum of Virginia
2500 West Broad Ave., Richmond, VA 23220; 804/257-1013

Science Museum of Western Virginia
1 Market Square, Roanoke, VA 24011; 703/343-7876

Virginia Living Museum
524 J. Clyde Morris Blvd., Newport News, VA 23601; 804/595-1900

Virginia Marine Science Museum
717 General Booth Blvd., Virginia Beach, VA 23451; 804/425-3474

District of Columbia

Capital Children's Museum
800 Third St., NE, Washington, DC 20002; 202/543-8600
Explorers Hall
17th and M Sts., NW, Washington, DC 20036; 202/857-7000
National Air and Space Museum
Independence Ave. & 7th St., Washington, DC 20560; 202/357-1504
The National Aquarium
14th St. & Constitution, NW, Washington, DC 20230; 202/377-2825
National Museum of American History
12th St. & Constitution, NW, Washington, DC 20560; 202/357-1300
National Museum of Natural History
10th St. & Constitution, NW, Washington, DC 20560; 202/357-2700
National Zoological Park
3001 Connecticut, NW, Washington, DC 20008; 202/673-4800

CANADA

National Museum of Science and Technology
1867 St. Laurent Blvd., Ottawa Terminal, Ottawa, Ontario, Canada
K1G−5A3, 613/991-3044
Ontario Science Centre
770 Don Mills Rd., Don Mills, Ontario, Canada M3C−1T3;
416/429-4100

Creating a Science "Tool Kit"

MEASURING EQUIPMENT
Clock (digital is best for accuracy)
Thermometer
Tape measure
Cooking measures—spoon sets, cup sets
Calipers (for measuring trees)
Weight set/balance scale (can be kitchen or bathroom type, or hanging type found in supermarkets)

ANIMAL EQUIPMENT
Aquarium, filter, pump, heater, light, etc. (for fish)
Nets (for catching fish, insects, etc.)
Cages, boxes, tubs
Food dishes, water bottles, exercisers, etc. (for rodents)
Terrarium (for rodents and reptiles)
Insect cages or jars
Bird-feeding station (hummingbird feeders, if appropriate)
Birdhouses

PLANT EQUIPMENT
Hand tools (trowel, etc.)
Large tools (spades, hoes, rakes, etc.)

Flat boxes, tubs, trays
Plant pots, boxes, egg cartons
Saucers, lids
Growing lights
Watering cans
Outdoor hose

GENERAL SCIENTIFIC EQUIPMENT

Pocket knife
Scissors
Tongs, tweezers, forceps
Geology hammer (or rock pick)
Magnifying glass
Mirror
Flashlight
Magnets (horseshoe and bar types)
Magnetic compass
Air pump
Mortar and pestle
Kitchen baster/suction device
Safety goggles
Eye droppers
Tongue depressors/Popsicle sticks

SPECIALIZED SCIENTIFIC EQUIPMENT

Dissecting kit
Portable greenhouse
Vacuum cleaner
Ice-cream freezer (crank type)
Food blender
Stethoscope
Kaleidoscope
Gears and geared devices
Clocks (to be taken apart)
Pulley and wheels
Lever devices
Binoculars
Telescope
Microscope

Pinwheels/windmills
Weather vane
Wind sock
Camera (preferably, Polaroid)
Ball bearings
Prisms
Sunglasses
Kites
Tape recorder
Record player
Radio

GENERAL MATERIALS

Plastic and paper bags
Paper rolls and spools
Cardboard tubes, carpet rolls
Newspapers
Paper and notebooks
Pencils and pens
Wax pencils
Gummed labels
Tape (both masking and cellophane)
Corks, plugs, stoppers, lids, etc.
Springs
Wire
Pipe cleaners, twist-tie wires
Rubber bands
String, yarn, fishing line, thread, rope, etc.
Kite string
Nails, tacks, screws, bolts, nuts
Washers (rubber and metal)
Steel wool
Sandpaper
Toothpicks
Filter paper; coffee filters
Wax paper, aluminum foil
Sponges
Cotton balls

Drinking straws (plastic is best)

Wax (paraffin, beeswax, or candle)

Household machine oil

Cleaning supplies (ammonia, bleach, detergent, etc.)

Cooking staples (sugar, flour, cornstarch, cooking oil, salt, vinegar, soda, etc.)

Blotting paper

Cheesecloth

Cardboard boxes

SCIENTIFIC SPECIMENS

Seaweed

Mosses, lichens

Seashells

Wool samples

Leather samples

Fossils

Rocks and pebbles

Soil samples

Real cork and sponge samples

Seedpods

Conifer cones

Seeds of all sorts

Bones

Horns and antlers

Eggs

Feathers

Fur samples

Natural fabrics and synthetic fabrics

Whole grains (wheat, oats, rye, rice, corn, etc.)

Edible seeds (sunflower, sesame, poppy, caraway, flax, etc.)

Dried fruits and vegetables (apricots, peaches, pears, prunes, apples, raisins, peas, beans, etc.)

6

Scientific Companies That Publish Science Catalogs and Distribute Teaching Tools

You can contact the following scientific companies by mail to find out what they offer in the way of teaching tools for teaching children science. Most offer free or inexpensive catalogs, newsletters, charts, posters, and other such items.

Bausch and Lomb
1400 N. Goodman St.
Rochester, NY 14602

Educational microscopes
for children

Carolina Biological Supply Co.
2700 York Rd.
Burlington, NC 27215

Biological specimens, posters,
newsletter

CEBCO
9 Kulick Rd.
Fairfield, NJ 07006

Science books and related
materials

Central Scientific Co. (CENCO)
2600 Kostner Ave.
Chicago, IL 60623

Science materials and equipment

Continental Press
Elizabethtown, PA 17022

Electricity experiments,
science booklets

Creative Publications, Inc.
P.O. Box 238
Palo Alto, CA 94302

Catalog of creative math and science manipulative materials

Edmund Scientific Company
7789 Edscorp Building
Barrington, NJ 08007

Astronomy materials, including star charts, planet finders, prisms, and free issues of *Astronomy News*

Estes Industries
P.O. Box 227
Penrose, CO 81240

Information on building model rockets, wind tunnels, etc.

Fisher Scientific Co.
4901 W. Lemoyne
Chicago, IL 60651

Information on educational and science materials

Hubbard Scientific Co.
1946 Raymond Dr.
Northbrook, IL 60062

Science media and materials

Jewel Industries
5005 W. Armitage Ave.
Chicago, IL 60639

Aquariums, animal cages, live specimens, etc.

Lab-Aids, Inc.
130 Wilbur Place
Bohemia, NY 11716

General science equipment and materials

NASA
400 Maryland Ave., SW
Washington, DC 20546

Information on the space shuttle and on what it takes to be an astronaut

OHAUS
29 Hanover Rd.
Florham Park, NJ 07932

Mathematical and science equipment

Sargent-Welch Scientific Co.
7300 N. Linder Ave.
Skokie, IL 60077

Science materials

Science Kit, Inc.
Tonowanda, NY 14150

General science materials and equipment

Science Research Associates, Inc.
259 East Erie St.
Chicago, IL 60611

"Inquiry Development Program" materials and films

Science Service
1719 North St., NW
Washington, DC 20036

Small kits of science materials for all sciences

Toys 'n Things
906 North Dale
St. Paul, MN 55103

Publishes *Teachables from Trashables: Homemade Toys That Teach*

APPENDIX

7

Mapping the Sciences: Which Science Should Your Child Learn?

The choice of which science your child should learn will, of course, depend on where his or her interests lie. This appendix was compiled to serve as a sort of "road map" to the sciences, giving you and your child some idea of the choices available. When I was growing up, one of the most confusing things for me concerning science was how all the sciences fit together and which discipline belonged to which science. A simple chart like the one that follows would have saved me many hours of wondering.

Many of the subdisciplines listed may be foreign to you, but a good encyclopedia will have at least a short description of what is involved in that aspect of the science.* Virtually all of the subdisciplines have been listed to give the reader a feeling for how vast and exciting the choices are. Science offers something for practically everyone!

To select a particular science to explore further, first read the encyclopedia descriptions of the topics on the list that follows, to see what seems most exciting. Then head for the library to check out a few books on that subject. There are books specifically for children on almost every science.

---

*The *Encyclopaedia Britannica* is the most thorough and accurate source and is best suited for adults, teenagers, and children with advanced learning skills. The *World Book Encyclopedia* and a couple of others are designed especially for children. However, if you are serious about teaching your child science properly, the *Britannica* is a necessity.

142

MATHEMATICS

ALGEBRA
ANALYSIS/CALCULUS
ARITHMETIC
GEOMETRY
MATRIX THEORY
NUMBER THEORY
PROBABILITY
SET THEORY
STATISTICS
TOPOLOGY
TRIGONOMETRY

PHYSICAL SCIENCES

AERODYNAMICS
ASTRONOMY
BIOCHEMISTRY
CELESTIAL MECHANICS
CHEMISTRY
COSMOLOGY
FLUID MECHANICS
INFRARED ASTRONOMY
MECHANICS
OPTICS
PHYSICS
QUANTUM MECHANICS
RADIO AND RADAR ASTRONOMY
STATISTICAL MECHANICS
THERMODYNAMICS
X-RAY ASTRONOMY

EARTH SCIENCES

ASTROGEOLOGY
BIOCLIMATOLOGY
BIOGEOCHEMISTRY
CHEMICAL HYDROLOGY
CLIMATOLOGY
DENDROCHRONOLOGY
ECONOMIC GEOLOGY
ENVIRONMENTAL GEOLOGY
GEOCHEMISTRY
GEOCHRONOLOGY
GEOHYDROLOGY
GEOMORPHOLOGY

GEOPHYSICS
HYDROLOGY
HYDROMETEOROLOGY
MARINE GEOLOGY
MARINE GEOPHYSICS
METEOROLOGY
MINERALOGY
OCEANOGRAPHY
PALEOCLIMATOLOGY
PALEOGEOGRAPHY
PALEOGEOLOGY
PALYNOLOGY
PEDOLOGY
PETROLOGY
SEDIMENTOLOGY
SEISMOLOGY
TECTONICS
VOLCANOLOGY

BIOLOGICAL SCIENCES

ANATOMY
BIOGEOGRAPHY
BIOLOGY
BIOPHYSICS
BOTANY
CYTOLOGY
ECOLOGY
EMBRYOLOGY
ENTOMOLOGY
ETHOLOGY
EUGENICS
EXOBIOLOGY
GENETIC ENGINEERING
GENETICS
HERPETOLOGY
HUMAN ECOLOGY
ICHTHYOLOGY
MAMMALOGY
MICROBIOLOGY
MORPHOLOGY
ORNITHOLOGY
PALEONTOLOGY
PALYNOLOGY
PARASITOLOGY

PHYSIOLOGY
PROTOZOOLOGY
TAXONOMY
ZOOLOGY

MEDICINE
AEROSPACE MEDICINE
DENTISTRY
ENDODONTICS
EPIDEMIOLOGY
HEMATOLOGY
NURSING
ORAL SURGERY

ORTHODONTICS
OSTEOPATHY
PEDODONTICS
PHARMACOLOGY
PHARMACY
PLASTIC SURGERY
PROSTHODONTICS
PSYCHIATRY
PUBLIC HEALTH
RADIOLOGY
SPORTS MEDICINE
SURGERY
TOXICOLOGY

SOCIAL SCIENCES

ANTHROPOLOGY (anthropological linguistics, ethnography, physical anthropology, cultural anthropology)

ECONOMICS (classical, institutional, Keynesian, econometrics, macroeconomics, microeconomics, managerial economics, welfare)

POLITICAL SCIENCE (public opinion, public law, public administration, political systems, international relations)

PSYCHOLOGY (Behavioral, clinical, comparative, developmental, educational, experimental, gestalt, humanistic, industrial, physiological, social)

SOCIOLOGY (criminology, demography, futurology, penology)

TECHNOLOGICAL SCIENCES
ACOUSTICAL ENGINEERING
AERONAUTICAL ENGINEERING
BIOENGINEERING
BIONICS
CHEMICAL ENGINEERING
CIVIL ENGINEERING
COMPUTER SCIENCE
ELECTRICAL ENGINEERING
INDUSTRIAL ENGINEERING
MECHANICAL ENGINEERING
NUCLEAR ENGINEERING
PETROLEUM ENGINEERING

I wish you good luck in helping your child to select the science that is most appropriate and exciting for him or her. There is nothing more valuable than a good education, as the English essayist, poet, and dramatist Joseph Addison noted in 1711:

> Education is a companion which no misfortune can depress, no crime can destroy, no enemy can alienate, no despotism can enslave. At home a friend, abroad an introduction, in solitude a solace, and in society an ornament. It chastens vice, it guides virtue, it gives, at once, grace and government to genius. Without it, what is man? A spendid slave, a reasoning savage.

Index

About the Author:

Michael Shermer is an Assistant Professor of Psychology at Glendale College in Glendale, California. He has a bachelor's degree in psychology (with a minor in biology) from Pepperdine University and a master's degree in experimental psychology from California State University, Fullerton. He is currently completing a Ph.D. in the history of science at Claremont Graduate School.

Professor Shermer teaches psychology, evolution, and the history of science. He has published papers in professional journals and has also presented papers at scientific and scholarly conferences. He is currently researching a book entitled *Evolution, Science, and Culture: Essays on the Cultural Heritage of Evolutionary and Scientific Thought.*

Michael Shermer also races bicycles, having enjoyed a career as an endurance cyclist as one of the founders of and four-time participant in the *Race Across America.* He has several published books on cycling and sports psychology, including *Psychling, Sport Cycling, Cycling, Endurance and Speed, The Woman Cyclist,* and *The RAAM Book.*